CO
TEN BOOM

CORRIE
TEN BOOM
WORLD WAR II HEROINE

SAM WELLMAN

BARBOUR
PUBLISHING

© 1995 by Sam Wellman

Print ISBN 978-1-61626-905-0

eBook Editions:
Adobe Digital Edition (.epub) 978-1-62029-648-6
Kindle and MobiPocket Edition (.prc) 978-1-62029-647-9

Material from the following books used by permission of Fleming H. Revell, a division of Baker Book House: Corrie ten Boom, *In My Father's House* © 1976; Carole C. Carlson, *Corrie ten Boom: Her Life, Her Faith* © 1983; Corrie ten Boom, *Father ten Boom* © 1978; Corrie ten Boom, *Prison Letters* © 1978.

All scripture quotations are taken from the King James Version of the Bible.

Cover illustration: Greg Copeland
Cover design: Kirk DouPonce

Published by Barbour Publishing, Inc., P.O. Box 719, Uhrichsville, Ohio 44683, www.barbourbooks.com

Our mission is to publish and distribute inspirational products offering exceptional value and biblical encouragement to the masses.

 Member of the
Evangelical Christian
Publishers Association

Printed in the United States of America.

CONTENTS

1.
JESUS IS HERE

The vaporizer on the small alcohol stove spewed a fog of camphor and water into the air of the dark bedroom. The vapor settled over Corrie ten Boom, who clutched a blanket over herself on a bed. Aches shadowed every movement of her body.

"Dear Jesus," she prayed, "let this pass."

Corrie ten Boom felt her years. It seemed as if until today she had never stopped long enough in all her fifty-two years to let age catch up with her. But more than age caught up with her today. Her prayer was a plea for many things to pass. Jesus had been in her heart for a very long time, and she hoped her fear was just momentary, just another unpleasant symptom of the flu.

"But everything has gone wrong lately," she muttered.

It seemed everyone in Holland must know the ten Booms were hiding fugitives in their house. After all, it was 1944. Holland had been infested by German soldiers for four years. The worst of all the Germans were the slithery Gestapo, the secret police of the Nazis. The ten Booms had been hiding Jews and Dutch boys in their house for two years. They never had less than seven fugitives living with them these desperate days. How much longer could their secret last before the dreaded Gestapo bashed on their door? The Gestapo struck at night like vipers. Their victims were groggy,

THE GESTAPO STRUCK AT NIGHT LIKE VIPERS.

unprepared—like Corrie felt now.

"Is it night or day?" She tried to focus her eyes.

She had slept in this very same bedroom in this very same house as long as she could remember. Her home was precious to her. The past was so wonderful that thinking about it softened her pain. Her thoughts drifted back. . . .

Yes. As far back as she could remember her home was *gezellig,* close and warm and cozy—smelling of soup and fresh bread, and sounding of soft laughter and the rustles of Mama and three aunts in long dresses. A five-year-old like Corrie could have a wonderful party with her doll Casperina under the dining room table. She could even creep down the steps into Papa's workroom behind his shop that faced Barteljorisstraat. Silently she sat and smelled his cigar and listened to clocks ticking and tocking like hundreds of heartbeats. She watched bearded Papa bent over his bench. Each time he placed some tiny thing in a watch he would pause and say, "Thank You, Lord," as gently as if he were talking to Corrie or Mama. That was Papa. God must have been right there with him.

Still, as gezellig as the home was, there were limits on the quantities of sound and activity that were correct and proper for a Dutch home in 1897. And to be allowed to explode beyond those limits, five-year-old Corrie had to play outside in the narrow alley. Her aunts with their tight-bunned hair seemed very happy when she asked for permission to play outside before she dashed into the alley. But Mama was not so happy.

Except on her sick days Mama's great wide blue eyes would appear in the dining room window again and again to check on her. Aunt Bep called Corrie the "baby" of the family. Corrie heard her say that while she was playing with Casperina under the table one day. Corrie didn't like to be called a baby. If another baby would just arrive she wouldn't be the baby any more. Aunt Anna had told her that when a baby is too small and weak to live in the cold world there is a special place under the mother's heart where the baby is warm and can grow. That's where Mama carried Corrie. Now if Mama would just carry another baby there Corrie would no longer be the baby.

Out in the alley, Corrie was not a baby. She was just one of many children who played there. Except for the town square and streets, which were bricked solid and overrun with grownups, there was little other open space in downtown Haarlem. The alleys were not much more than sun-starved slits among tall buildings, but they did have precious space. And they weren't dangerous like the streets. It was rare for a wagon or a rider to intrude into the alley.

"And who can't hear wheels rumbling or a horse clopping up the potholed alley anyway?" reasoned Corrie's papa with worried Mama.

Corrie skipped rope by herself on her sturdy legs or joined the other children to play bowl-the-hoop or a game with a ball and stones called *bikkelen*. Even blue-skinned Sammy was out there almost every day, bundled up and slumped in a wheelchair. It was hard to include him in much more than an occasional game of tag, when he was home base. Sammy's moment came when Corrie's sister Nollie—the *moedertje*, the "little mother"—came home from school. She would start to play with the other children but in no time at all she was pushing Sammy's wheelchair, mothering him.

Nollie's return expanded Corrie's world. Corrie would cry, "Let's go to the square!"

While Sammy slumped even more in his wheelchair and began grumbling about potholes rattling his bones, Nollie would go inside to get permission to go to the square with Corrie. The two sisters would hold hands and hurry down the alley. On Barteljoris-straat, horses pulled trolley cars, clanging toward the town square only half a block distant. From the square itself, rich bells bonged and pealed. They would whisk down the narrow sidewalk past tall, dark brick buildings until Corrie saw the gothic spire of Saint Bavo's towering over the square. The girls would find a bench and watch grownups strolling through the square or hurrying to their trolley.

"Who is Laurens Coster again?" Corrie would ask Nollie.

Nollie would glance at the statue that held center stage in the square.

"Laurens Coster was a Haarlemite who invented the printing press. Pay no mind to what ignorant people say about some German called Gutenberg." Nollie's face had that special hardheaded look of the Dutch: *eigenwijs*. She was stubborn.

So was Corrie. "I'll pay no mind."

The square was crowded with tailors' businesses and shops of housewares and other specialties of all kinds. Many people bustled in and out of the shops. Nestled against Saint Bavo's was the fish market. Across a tiny street was the butcher's hall. On one side of the square was the town hall. Three times a week the area was choked with farmers walking in wooden *klompen*, selling fruit and vegetables to the women of Haarlem, who wore long black dresses and black bonnets. Nollie would say, "Papa says our Dutch farmers are like no other farmers in the world. They took their land from the very sea."

When the square was too crowded with farmers, the sisters would find cousin Dot, who lived next to Saint Bavo's, and sneak inside the great cathedral. Uncle Arnold was an usher of the church. Inside was a colossal golden organ that sounded as heavenly as it looked. The cathedral always made Corrie think of heaven.

Sometimes they ventured a short way down Damstraat to the Spaarne River. It was a bouquet of colorful boats. Their pilots bragged they could take Corrie anyplace in Holland on a boat. It was no surprise to her. She couldn't go more than a few blocks from home in any direction without coming to a canal or the river. And of course if she walked west of Haarlem with Papa, in not much more than an hour's time she faced the mighty North Sea.

> **THE PILOTS BRAGGED THEY COULD TAKE CORRIE ANYPLACE IN HOLLAND ON A BOAT.**

But the two sisters didn't always leave the alley to go to the town square. Sometimes while they played, Corrie would hear a commotion from the direction away from Barteljorisstraat and plead, "Oh, please, Nollie, let's go see!"

Nollie didn't ask permission. "We'll only look."

Nollie would take her cautiously down the alley to Smedestraat. There they might see the bad-smelling man called Crazy Thys, whirling in confusion, teased on all sides by children. But lately it was Corrie, not seven-year-old Nollie, who scolded the children for their cruelty. Or they might see police scooping up drunkards in front of saloons and dragging them off to the station house. The saloons on Smedestraat always made Corrie think of hell.

Their home seemed balanced between a world tainted with sights and sounds of hell on one side and a world blessed with sights and sounds of heaven on the other side. But heaven and hell were real places. She knew this because Papa read the Bible aloud to them every day at exactly eight thirty in the morning and nine-forty-five at night. In the Bible, Jesus spoke of heaven and He spoke of hell. So they were real places. Only a few weeks ago, Mama had asked Corrie to invite Jesus into her heart and she had. Before Jesus came into her heart, Corrie would never have scolded the children for teasing Crazy Thys. She saw how surprised Nollie was at her sudden courage.

It wasn't that long ago—she may have been four—when she had sung Aunt Jans's own made-up song as "I should just like to *peek*, Savior, into the beautiful Father-House," instead of "I should just like to *come*, Savior, into the beautiful Father-House." Aunt Anna had laughed at her mistake, but it was no mistake. Corrie just wanted to peek—that was all. But that was before Jesus came into her heart.

It wasn't that long ago that on one of their walks she and Nollie were bowled over by a nasty man on a bicycle. Spattered with mud, they ran inside the house. Everyone came running to the squalling Nollie. While they wiped the mud off Nollie and hugged away her hurts, timid Corrie stood aside in a corner, silent and trembling, her hurts unnoticed. But that was before Jesus came into her heart.

And not long before that, she and Nollie had gone with Mama when she took fresh bread to Mrs. Hoog one block away. Right in the midst of several unusually quiet grownups in a room was a crib with a baby in it. The smooth white face with delicate lashes over the closed eyes looked sweeter than any doll. Nollie gently touched the cheek. So Corrie touched the tiny hand. It was ice cold!

"Baby is dead!" gasped Corrie.

That night in bed she clutched Nollie's nightgown tighter than ever. Death. A baby. If an innocent baby that looked sweeter than any doll could die, then why couldn't anyone die at any time? Even Mama. Even Papa. Even Corrie herself! If Papa didn't talk to her about Jesus every night would she ever be able to sleep again? Would she ever let go of Nollie's nightgown?

And yet one day not long ago, as Corrie played under the dining room table, Mama had suggested she invite Jesus into her heart. After that she no longer clutched Nollie's nightgown at night. Jesus was not just in the Bible. He was real. He was alive inside her heart. She was as sure of that as anything in her world. Mama said Jesus would never let her down. Unless, of course, Corrie forgot He was there.

IF PAPA DIDN'T TALK TO HER ABOUT JESUS EVERY NIGHT WOULD SHE EVER BE ABLE TO SLEEP AGAIN?

2.
SCHOOL DAYS

Corrie was six when one morning came that she dreaded. Summer was over, and more than that was over. Betsie, her oldest sister, who seemed almost grown-up because she had something called anemia and had to sit around knitting, was in the bedroom with her and Nollie.

Nollie blurted, "I won't wear the hat Aunt Jans bought me!" She glared at the wide-brimmed brown bonnet on the wardrobe. Lavender roses of velvet were clustered on it.

Betsie soothed her, "You must wear a hat. . . ."

"Mrs. van Dyver at the millinery shop gave me this," said Nollie, almost breathlessly. She pulled a hat box from under the bed and opened it. Inside was a tiny pillbox hat of fur with a chinstrap of blue satin.

"How precious," said Betsie.

Now was the perfect time for Corrie to explain her plan to her sisters. "I've decided," rattled Corrie, "it would really be best if I stayed home to help Aunt Anna. Why start school at all?"

In a tired voice, Betsie said, "Let me help you lace your shoes, Corrie." And she used a button hook on Corrie's high-topped shoes.

Corrie said, "Did you hear me? I've decided—"

Nollie interrupted her, "Don't forget your hat, Corrie."

Corrie looked at the gray hat Nollie had worn to school last year. "You don't understand. I've decided. . ." She stopped. Her sisters had already left the bedroom to go downstairs to breakfast.

They wouldn't listen. She had never been to school one day in her life, and she didn't intend to start today. She saw the clock on the dresser. It was ten after eight! She grabbed the floppy gray hat, even though she had no use for it, and ran down two flights of stairs. In the dining room she slapped it on a peg on the wall next to the pillbox hat and hopped into her chair.

SHE HAD NEVER BEEN TO SCHOOL ONE DAY IN HER LIFE, AND SHE DIDN'T INTEND TO START TODAY.

Papa was at the table. Sour Aunt Bep sat there, too. Mama and Aunt Anna were serving. Brother Peter, eleven and always hungry, impatiently cracked his knuckles and eyed the pot of yellow cheese and a platter with a large, round loaf of fresh bread. Everyone was at breakfast but Aunt Jans. Corrie saw the looks exchanged between her sisters, Nollie and Betsie. Could it be a miracle? Perhaps Aunt Jans really was sick for once. Nollie could wear her nice hat to school after all.

And better yet, Corrie could tell Papa and Mama now of her wonderful plan. . . .

But Mama spoke first. "Aunt Jans is making a tonic in the kitchen." Corrie listened with deaf ears as Mama explained why Aunt Jans didn't feel well. There was always some reason.

Anger suddenly scattered her thoughts. It was Aunt Jans's angry voice. "A well-brought-up girl's hat should have a brim!" She was glaring at the pillbox hat!

Mama jumped up to hover over the pot of cheese. She sniffed at it suspiciously. Papa looked bewildered. Aunt Jans frowned at the cheese. Something wrong with the cheese? She would pass judgment. She focused on the cheese. Yes, she judged, the cheese was all right. One couldn't be too careful. One of her friends her own age had died from a fish gone bad! Papa said grace. Aunt Jans looked unsettled all through breakfast. What was it she had been saying before she inspected the cheese?

There was so much commotion and breakfast tasted so delicious, Corrie forgot something, too. Then she remembered! Now she would announce her wonderful plan. . . .

The door to the alley opened. "The workers are here," said Peter impatiently.

Corrie joined the others at the table in exchanging a friendly *"Goedemorgen"* with the clock man and the errand boy who worked in the shop for Papa.

"Sit down, friends." Papa put on his rimless glasses and opened the Bible. He read a psalm in his slow, deep voice.

The instant Papa gently closed the Bible, Peter jumped from the table, snatched his cap from a peg, leaped down the five steps of the stairway, and bolted out the door into the alley. Nollie was right behind him.

As Betsie gracefully followed them down the stairs, Aunt Jans blinked at the pegs. She sighed. "Nollie forgot to wear the hat I bought her."

"That's not the worst of it!" Mama's eyes widened at Corrie. "Nollie forgot to take Corrie with her."

Thank God Nollie forgot, thought Corrie. *It's not too late to explain.* Corrie said, "I've decided that it would really be best if I stayed home to help Aunt Anna. Why start school at all?"

Papa rose from the table. "Corrie doesn't want to go alone on her first day to school." He took her hand in one hand and the gray hat from the peg with the other.

It was only long after Papa had firmly removed the hand she tried to anchor to the railing on the stairs and had tugged her to school that she remembered Jesus. He was in her heart. She asked Him for courage. Almost at that moment she saw her cousin Dot in the classroom. They were already good friends. For years they would go to school together. Corrie would not be alone.

School was not without peril. One terrible recess, Corrie stepped on a blue ceramic tile that the headmaster had warned all the students not to touch. Out of nowhere, a ham of a hand popped her in the face. She had never even been spanked before. The headmaster's slap was the most humiliating moment of her life. The horror burned into her memory like a photograph: a girl in a red dress and white apron stood in front of her, and there was a green gate—then the vicious slap, a punishment a thousand times worse than her "sin."

There were dangers away from school, too. Once when Dot was busy doing something else, Corrie accepted a teenager's invitation to play in the dunes west of town. Once hidden in the dunes he began to teach her a new game. He moved his hands all over her. His game was no fun at all, and Corrie felt her skin crawl with disgust. She pulled away from him. She told him that Mama and Jesus would think the game was dirty. He was angry then contrite. So she promised him not to tell anyone. But she babbled the whole story to Mama later in a fever. Mama thanked Jesus for being with Corrie and protecting her always. Then they prayed for Jesus to clean the filth from the teenager's heart and mind.

By the time Corrie was ten, she had the nickname *Kees*. It was a boy's name because she was a tomboy. Betsie was a tall, delicate, sloe-eyed seventeen-year-old with thick chestnut hair. Nollie

BY THE TIME CORRIE WAS TEN, SHE HAD THE NICKNAME *KEES*. IT WAS A BOY'S NAME BECAUSE SHE WAS A TOMBOY.

was twelve, solid and blonde, with a square face and nose so perfect they belonged on a princess. Both sisters turned the heads of boys like magnets. But then there was Corrie. The pretty little girl lengthened and strengthened in all the wrong places. She became pigeon-toed and high-hipped. Her lips were wide and so thin they were a cartoon. Her jaw got stubborn and never softened. Her eyes, turned down on the corners, would have seemed perpetually sorrowful if she hadn't smiled so much. Such slight differences between beautiful and homely!

Perhaps Corrie had known it was coming for a long time. Betsie kept her doll Emma so well dressed no one would question why the doll was named after the mother of the Netherlands' queen. Nollie's doll was just as sovereign. And then there was Corrie's Casperina. Casperina had a cracked head and missing fingers. Still, she looked better than could be expected for a doll that was held carelessly by one leg and dragged with head and arms thumping up and down the stairs. Corrie didn't care how Casperina looked, she loved her and Jesus loved her.

But realizing she was not attractive to boys seemed to make her ornery. Was she trying to get attention that way? She and Dot had some very good times—before and after school. Once Dot found a dime broken into two pieces. They carefully pieced it back together on the counter top at the sweet shop to pay for ten pieces of candy. They were running out of the shop as the dime disintegrated in the owner's fingers. Another time they snowballed top hats off stuffy gentlemen on the sidewalk. What a great trick it was to play the sweet little angels and retrieve the top hats from the street. As she and Dot conscientiously brushed the snow off the splendid hats, they acted as indignant as the gentlemen as their outraged eyes searched the streets for the villains.

But she and Dot had the most fun in Saint Bavo's Cathedral. For as long as Corrie could remember, she had gone there every Sunday morning for the service. She put on her Christmas dress and trudged behind Papa and the ladies. Some said the organ in the cathedral had five thousand pipes, but who could count them? High above the pews hung tiny bells in the form of ships. The cavernous cathedral, which was always cool during the service and in winter bone chilling, seemed warm when she played there with Dot after school.

Dot actually lived in a little house for the usher nestled into the side of the cathedral. Dot and Corrie could play inside the vast interior everywhere but the pulpit. They played tag around the massive pillars. They hid in closets during hide-and-seek. They slipped through the swinging half doors on the pews and defended themselves against Napoleon.

They opened closed doors and climbed the Matterhorn on winding staircases. They clomped up the very steps Mozart climbed into the organ loft, and they pretended to play the colossal organ with its sixty-eight stops. The great stone-and-brick interior echoed with their screams of delight. Once in a while

> "PLEASE, CHILDREN, THERE ARE GRAVES OF SAINTS BELOW YOU."

Uncle Arnold would shush them for a moment with, "Please, children, there are graves of saints below you." But that didn't slow them down for long.

Corrie loved to scheme and make plans. It was a trait of everyone in her family, but it amazed her girl friends who did not know that. "Another plan?" asked one friend. "How many plans do you have, Corrie?"

"Sixteen."

"But that's silly," scoffed the girl. "You can't carry out sixteen plans."

"How many plans do you have?"

"Why, I have none yet."

"Then if I carry out only two of my plans that's a lot more than none!"

But Corrie might have been better off if she had not carried out some of her plans. Once at school she wanted to show off her watch. She was the only one of sixty in her class who had one. As members of her own family were always organizing things, she hatched a plan. She urged her classmates to smuggle their caps and hats into the room and hide them under their desks. She would signal at precisely two o'clock, and they would all pop their caps and hats on their heads to astonish the teacher. The teacher wouldn't punish the whole class. But at two o'clock, when Corrie waved her hand, popped her blue and white sailor hat on her head, and looked around triumphantly, the other students just gazed at her with cow's eyes. She realized the joke was on her as the teacher angrily sent her away to the headmaster.

That night Nollie was aghast. "Papa would be so ashamed that you used your watch that way."

"That's not all," admitted Corrie. "I didn't go to the headmaster. I hid in a coat closet until school got out."

She had never seen Nollie so upset. "Do you remember the line that is repeated over and over in Psalm 107, Corrie? 'Then they cried unto the LORD in their trouble, and he delivered them out of their distresses.' You had better do just that!"

So that's what Corrie did the rest of the evening. She cried out to the Lord in her trouble. She prayed and prayed. The next day she almost crawled to the headmaster. He didn't punish her at all for her "sin." Was that a tiny smile on the corner of his lips? The outside world was so unpredictable. Or was it her prayer?

She kept telling herself she didn't care how she looked. And so what if she did act like a boy once in a while? Once she skipped home from school smashing big black flies against a wooden fence. She smashed more than one. If a boy saw her smashing flies, he would certainly think Corrie ten Boom was quite the adventurous rascal. Then she heard the deep voice behind her, "What a joy to meet my youngest daughter here on the street." It was Papa. There wasn't the slightest reprimand in his voice, and at that moment she was embarrassed. She felt dirty. When they walked through the door from the alley, he said, "I know you will want to wash your hands before you see your mother."

The love in her home finally seemed to put out the fire of Corrie's rebellion.

> **THE LOVE IN HER HOME PUT OUT THE FIRE OF CORRIE'S REBELLION.**

3.
NATURAL ORGANIZERS

Corrie began to care about her manners. She didn't want to be a tomboy. She knew she would never be beautiful, and she would never have the desire or flair for elegant clothes that Betsie and Nollie had. But she did want to be a young lady. No one could long resist the love of a family so grounded in Christ.

The outside world made her cherish home life more. Nothing unfair happened at home. Even Aunt Bep's sour outlook on life was only a mild irritation. Mama made her understand that much of Aunt Bep's unhappiness was only talk. Bitter talk was certainly a sin, warned about in the Proverbs, and in the book by James— oh, bitter talk had been a sin for thousands of years. But it need only be a small sin if smothered by love so it would not spread. Corrie understood Aunt Bep was to be tolerated, even loved.

Mama wondered aloud to Corrie, "Can any of us understand what might have happened in your Aunt Bep's thirty-five years as a domestic servant that might have caused her peculiar sourness?"

On the other hand, the peculiar ways of Aunt Jans were amusing. She was imperious and demanding but also generous. Once she came into some money, and her first act was to go out and buy presents for everyone in the family. Aunt Jans would never hoard the money for herself. Her husband, Hendrick Wildeboer, who had died young, had been a minister. Aunt Jans still ministered in her own way. She was well-known around Haarlem for the fiery tracts she wrote. One of her milder tracts sternly warned its recipient:

> *Have you never introduced Jesus to someone else? Then I doubt that you know Him. Jesus has said, "I say unto you, Whosoever shall confess me before men, him shall the Son of man also confess before the angels of God: But he that denieth me before men shall be denied before the angels of God" (Luke 12:8–9).*

Then there was wise Aunt Anna. Corrie's prospects were so poor when she was born prematurely that Mama wrote later: "Nearly dead, she looked bluish white, and I never saw anything so pitiful. Nobody thought she would live." It was Aunt Anna who took Corrie—who had come too soon from Mama's womb—and carried her wrapped in her apron snug against the warmth of her plump belly, as if she still were in the womb. Aunt Anna was the one who kept the house spotless and the soup on the stove. Aunt Anna was the one Papa paid one guilder a week, only to have to ask for its return before the week was out. Aunt Anna was the one who added a sash or ribbon to Corrie's Christmas dress so it would look a little different on every Sunday and every special occasion as she wore it for the obligatory year.

AUNT JANS WAS WELL KNOWN AROUND HAARLEM FOR THE FIERY TRACTS SHE WROTE.

Corrie's sisters and brother were the best of friends. Willem was witty, but too often lapsed into seriousness, even gloom. Nollie was the strong sister. Of all the children, she was the most "normal," rarely ill or in trouble. Betsie was a sleepy-eyed beauty but had resolved never to marry because she had anemia. Marriage would destroy her. One had to look no further than Mama to see how bearing children could break a frail woman down.

Not that Mama ever seemed to regret it. Although barely forty years old, she lived in white-knuckled pain from gallstones. For several years, when the pain became too intense, she resorted to surgery. But after she had a minor stroke, the doctor gave her bad news: The surgery was too dangerous now; she just had to bear the pain of the gallstones. She never acted the martyr, but always the peacemaker. It was Mama who understood what was in someone's mind in a flash and smoothed things over before anyone else even realized what was happening. It was Mama who knitted baby clothes or wrote cheery messages for shut-ins—often from her invalid's bed!

PAPA'S FATHER, WILLEM, STARTED A SOCIETY FOR ISRAEL IN 1844 WHEN IT WAS UNPOPULAR TO BEFRIEND THE JEWS.

And then there was Papa, so well known as the best watchmaker in Holland that young men came from all over Europe to ask to be his apprentices. Papa always tried to accommodate them. But he was much more than a superb watchmaker. How he loved the Jews, God's chosen people. He came from a long line of ten Booms who were never afraid to take God's side as revealed in the Bible. Papa's grandfather Gerrit lost his job as a gardener because he spoke up against the dictator Napoleon. Papa's father, Willem, the original watchmaker at Barteljorisstraat, started a Society for Israel—a fellowship to pray for the Jews—in 1844 when it was unpopular to befriend the Jews.

Papa's love for the Jews matured in his first years as a watchmaker in the poor Jewish section of Amsterdam. He read the Old Testament—their Talmud—with them and even celebrated their Sabbath and holy days. He lived fifteen fruitful years in Amsterdam. He met Mama there. All the ten Boom children were born there. Aunt Anna and Aunt Bep were already living with him in Amsterdam.

Then Papa got a letter from his father, Willem, in Haarlem:

> *I am living one day at a time. God's goodness is eternal, and His faithfulness from generation to generation. I am so much enjoying the presence of the Lord, and I wait for Him. My suitcases are packed.*

Soon Papa returned to Haarlem. His father Willem died, and his mother needed help with the shop.

Papa accepted God's love, and he loved everyone. Like Jesus, he told parables on many occasions. One summer Corrie was returning with Papa on the train from Amsterdam, where he bought watch parts and carried back the official time from the Naval Observatory. This particular day she wasn't enjoying the fields of yellow and red tulips that surrounded Haarlem. She was gathering her courage to ask him a question that had troubled her ever since she read a poem at school. Finally she said in a low voice, "Papa, what is sex sin?"

He said, "When we get to Haarlem, will you carry my bag of watch parts from the station to our house?"

"No! The bag is too heavy for me."

"Yes. And I would be a poor papa to ask his young daughter to carry such a heavy load. It's the same with knowledge. Some knowledge is too heavy for you to carry now. You must trust me to carry the meaning of 'sex sin' for you until you are ready."

Another time she told Papa she was not only afraid of dying, but she was afraid someone in the family would die. After all, Mama and Jans both were sick a lot. How could she bear such pain?

Papa asked her, "When we take the train to Amsterdam, when do I give you the ticket?"

"Just before we get on the train."

"And so God will give you the courage to carry the pain when the time comes for someone to die. Until then you should not carry the pain. God does not want you to."

Before and *after* every meal Papa would ask God to bless the queen. He ended grace with, "Let soon come the day that Jesus, Your beloved Son, comes on the clouds of heaven. Amen." He never stopped reminding everyone that Christ was going to return.

Papa made sure the ten Booms didn't neglect what Haarlem had to offer. Right in the town hall hung paintings by Holland's masters of light, Vermeer, Rembrandt, and Haarlem's own Frans Hals. The masters reminded Corrie of the "Golden Age" of Holland and the terrible price they paid for it. Almost the very year Hals was born, thirty thousand Spaniards besieged Haarlem, defended by William the Silent and three thousand men. After seven months, each side had lost almost half its men.

"We who successfully resisted the Spaniards became Holland. Those

> **"GOD WILL GIVE YOU THE COURAGE TO CARRY THE PAIN WHEN THE TIME COMES. UNTIL THEN YOU SHOULD NOT CARRY THE PAIN."**

whose resistance failed became Belgium," joked Papa. That was as nasty as Papa ever got.

It was the sensitive Betsie who helped Corrie understand the groups of burgher guards and Haarlem corporations painted by Frans Hals. Each individual was bathed in light, caught in a fleeting moment hundreds of years before, somehow more real than the gawkers in the town hall. Could Corrie ever forget the *Regentesses of the Old Men's Almshouse*? Not only did Hals create his masterpiece at the age of eighty, Betsie told her, but it was of a group of powerful women!

Every time there was a concert, all the ten Booms but Mama would traipse to the concert hall, not to go inside, but to gather in the alley outside the hall with other music lovers too poor to buy tickets. The glorious music came billowing right out the stage door to those willing to stand for hours in the chilly night.

It seemed that every evening at home blossomed with activity. The family gathered on the second floor, in Aunt Jans's rooms, crammed with huge furniture she brought with her after her Hendrik died. A favorite pastime was reading aloud wonderful books by writers like Charles Dickens or Louisa May Alcott. Once, Corrie was so inspired she secretly labored over her own masterpiece. It was a magnificent tale of the adventures of Corrie, Dot, their friends, and no parents. She learned the hard way not to flaunt her manuscript. Betsie was brutally frank about its flaws. Corrie angrily hid the manuscript in the attic, and by the time she thought of it again it had been critiqued into shreds by mice.

Often the family would sing. They learned to sing everything from hymns to the Bach chorale *"Seid froh die Weil."* Willem sang tenor, Nollie soprano, and Corrie alto. Another favorite was Bible study combined with language study. That was one of the ways Corrie learned to read English and German almost as well as her native

Dutch. Mama would read a passage in Dutch. Willem would read the same passage in Hebrew or Greek. Papa or Betsie would read it in German. Nollie would read it in French. And Corrie would read the same passage in English.

"A penny in the blessing box for your coming," gushed Mama when guests arrived, and she would put a penny for the missionaries in a small metal box in the dining room. Every time the family was blessed in some way, this was her way of showing thanks to God. The guests were very flattered, too, because the ten Booms did not have an abundance of pennies. Guests would bring flutes and violins and all kinds of instruments to play in Aunt Jans's front room, where she had an upright piano. Aunt Jans even began inviting soldiers she saw loitering in the streets. One soldier was such a talented musician she talked him into giving Nollie and Corrie lessons on her pump organ.

It seemed every member of the family was a natural organizer. Soon Aunt Jans organized a soldier's center and raised funds for a building of their own. She went there herself to give Bible lessons and sing hymns. Corrie sang there, too. Even solos. Once she finished a song with the line "And the sheep that went astray was me."

The soldiers laughed. One asked, "How could such a young lady have gone astray?"

Corrie began to suspect that her past sins were not so large after all. She said, "Well, I did give my heart to Jesus when I was five."

The soldier looked sad. "How much better it is to find the shepherd as a little child than to have to stumble through life as I have, always seeking Him."

Aunt Anna was an organizer, too. She organized a club for servant girls. The poor innocents needed encouragement. They were often alone and preyed upon. Every Wednesday, she would meet with her girls for Bible study and hymns. And if one of her girls got in "trouble" Aunt Anna couldn't have been more heartbroken if the girl were her own daughter. Papa would try to console his sister-in-law, "You must not bear all this yourself, Anna. Remember what Peter said: 'Cast all your care upon him, for he careth for you.'"

Papa organized too. He published a little magazine for watchmakers. He was always involved in civic events such as the annual parade for the queen's birthday. And every week when he visited the houses of rich Haarlemites to wind their clocks, he would adjourn afterwards with the servants for Bible lessons. One just couldn't live in Christ without wanting to help one and all. And sometimes it was necessary to organize to get started.

ONE COULDN'T LIVE IN CHRIST WITHOUT WANTING TO HELP ONE AND ALL.

By the time Corrie was fourteen, she had a perspective on life that never changed. She had Jesus in her heart. She was a lady. She loved Holland and the queen. She knew a good family was a wonderful blessing not to be neglected, yet she still had to cope outside the family. The world outside could not be avoided, but she knew that success or failure outside in the world must not interfere with the family.

But she was not prepared for a broken heart.

4.
A FAILED VENTURE

Corrie was fourteen years old when she met Karel. Willem brought him home from college for one of Mama's celebrations. Whether they celebrated a marriage or an anniversary or a birthday, Corrie could not remember. All she remembered from that occasion was tall, blonde Karel. A young man of nineteen like Willem, he smoked a cigar like Papa. Karel was polite, but his deep brown eyes remained aloof.

It was not unusual for Corrie to be struck by love. She had loved every boy in her class at one time or another. Of course, none of them knew it. She was too shy and much too sure of her homeliness. But this love for Karel was different. Here he was right in their home. That familiarity made him special, as if he, like her family, cared nothing about how she looked but cared only about what was in her heart.

Nollie, of course, had barely noticed him. "Karel? What did he look like?" she asked later. Nollie was used to being the one noticed.

"He was heavenly," mooned Corrie.

Thus began a time in her life when Corrie was glad to be female. How she liked romance stories now. It seemed she was in the public library every day checking out romantic novels. Betsie raised an eyebrow more than once at her voracious reading of romances, but even Betsie did not catch on that Corrie craved them so much she read the most popular of them three times: in Dutch, in English, in German. *Studying the Bible is not the only way to learn other languages,* she told herself. Still, she wasn't going to brag about it to Papa.

Two years later, Nollie and Corrie decided to visit Willem at his university. Leiden was no more than a short train ride south along the dunes. Corrie tried to calm herself as the train rumbled along. She must not expect too much. Karel probably wouldn't even be there. Besides, how many times before had she mooned over a boy only to discover in the light of day that the boy was truly a monster? She must be more like Nollie—just be nonchalant and let things happen. But how could she be calm when her heart was beating like the North Sea crashing against the dikes?

> HOW MANY TIMES HAD SHE MOONED OVER A BOY ONLY TO DISCOVER THAT THE BOY WAS TRULY A MONSTER?

Willem greeted them on the fourth floor of a private home where he roomed. It seemed like only moments until Karel and three other men appeared in Willem's room.

It was that moment that Karel won Corrie's heart. Somewhere in the exchange of pleasant introductions he said, "Why, of course. We already know each other."

Was he looking at Nollie? No, he seemed to looking at Corrie! Her romance novels failed her. She could not think of a single word to reply.

During the conversation it was Nollie who blithely discussed the prospects for conquering the North Pole and the new theory of relativity with these college men. After all, she was in normal school already, studying to be a teacher. She didn't feel inferior to them in any way. Nollie never did.

But Corrie sat there, paralyzed.

When Karel looked right at her and asked her if she was going to normal school next year herself, Corrie blurted, "No, I'm staying home with Mama and Aunt Anna."

Later as they returned home on the train, her answer lingered with her, childishly weak. Yet she was needed at home more than ever. Aunt Bep had tuberculosis. The poor woman lay in her room most of the time now and coughed. Faithful sweet Aunt Anna alone tended to her, so no others would be exposed to the germs. Mama was not strong either. And Aunt Jans was just Aunt Jans. Aunt Anna did need help, but Corrie really wasn't sure if she wanted to stay at home. Nollie wasn't going to stay at home. Oh why was Corrie so unsure of her plans after sixteen years? And why couldn't she express herself?

And would she see Karel again? Could she even think the impossible? Oh, she realized he could not marry for many years. He and Willem had the same goal: to be ordained as Protestant ministers. A kind young man like Karel would not want to tie a girl's hands for years and years. But she could hope.

She finished secondary school and began working at home. She was not happy. She felt hot and weak. Surely it was her indecision. Once when the doctor made his regular call on Aunt Bep, Mama asked him, "Can you examine Corrie? She seems feverish to me."

"CORRIE DOES HAVE A FEVER. SHE HAS TUBERCULOSIS."

In far too short a time the doctor said, "Corrie does have a fever. She has tuberculosis." Her future was yanked away from her as cruelly as a fish suddenly hooked and yanked from the North Sea!

The doctor ordered bed rest immediately. Bed rest was a stunning blow. Corrie's life seemed barely started. At least Aunt Bep had gone out into the world for thirty-five years. How could God do this to her? And how could Aunt Bep have infected her? At what moment had the germs leaped from her mouth into Corrie's lungs? How could this be happening?

She hid her bitterness. In a house of the chronically sick, such as Aunt Bep, Aunt Jans, and Mama, how could she complain? She didn't want to be sour like Aunt Bep, but tuberculosis for people with little money was a death sentence. Only an expensive sanitarium and special care could save a victim of this dreaded lung disease.

Who counseled her? Was it Papa? Or was it in her own feverish hysteria that she quoted Paul's litany of miseries from 2 Corinthians 11?

> *Are they ministers of Christ? (I speak as a fool) I am more; in labours more abundant, in stripes above measure, in prisons more frequent, in deaths oft. Of the Jews five times received I forty stripes save one. Thrice was I beaten with rods, once was I stoned, thrice I suffered shipwreck, a night and a day I have been in the deep; in journeyings often, in perils of waters, in perils of robbers, in perils by mine own countrymen, in perils by the heathen, in perils in the city, in perils in the wilderness, in perils in the sea, in perils among false brethren; in weariness and painfulness, in watchings often, in hunger and thirst, in fastings often, in cold and nakedness.*

It was definitely Corrie who responded testily, "What is the point?"

"The point, dearest Corrie," answered a voice, "is that it is an honor to suffer for Christ."

Willem came by to sit with her. His exams were coming up. He had her drill him on theology, and he left some books with her. She passed the time reading books about church history. She studied her Bible. She read Paul and his never-ending trials. She found strength in the gospels.

She prayed, "Deliver me from this affliction, Lord."

She began to sense the living Christ. She prayed more and more. Soon she was praying for hours every day, but she had to keep telling herself she was not losing hope because deep in her heart she felt doomed. And as if she did not have enough to worry about, she developed a pain in her stomach.

She had been in bed five months when the doctor paid one of his regular visits to his patients in the ten Boom house. "How are you doing, Corrie?" he asked routinely. Corrie pressed the right side of her abdomen. "I have a pain here, doctor."

He poked and watched her wince. "You have appendicitis."

After the operation, her fever vanished. Corrie was perfectly healthy. She had never had tuberculosis at all!

AFTER THE OPERATION, HER FEVER VANISHED. SHE HAD NEVER HAD TUBERCULOSIS AT ALL!

The time in bed had solidified Corrie's flabby plans about getting out into the world. She began normal school and eagerly sought things to do outside the home. Her friend Mina talked her into telling Bible stories in Mina's class in a Christian school for children. Unsure of herself, Corrie asked Betsie's advice. Betsie had a perfect solution. Corrie would polish her technique in Betsie's Sunday school class first.

What a revelation. Her first time in front of children Corrie exhausted the story of Jesus feeding the five thousand in five minutes! Without a moment's hesitation, as if it had been planned, Betsie took up the story. She made the story come alive. Where were people sitting? Where had they come from? Did Jesus speak to them from the bottom of the hill or the top? What did the sea of Galilee look like? What were the people thinking before the miracle? What did they think after the miracle?

After that Corrie realized Betsie really did know how to tell a story. It was as if she painted a wonderful detailed picture, like one of the old masters. When Corrie praised her, Betsie simply replied that she had been telling stories to her Sunday school class for ten years.

So Corrie perfected her technique in Betsie's class then began to tell Bible stories in Mina's class, always remembering Betsie's flair for telling a story so it came alive. Corrie continued her studies in normal school and became more confident outside the home. Now she definitely wanted to leave home, but she felt guilty. They needed her so much.

She asked her own Bible teacher Mrs. van Lennep, "Am I wrong to want to leave home when they can use my help?"

"To want to leave home is natural. Actually to leave may be wrong or right. Perhaps you will never have a chance to leave, Corrie. If something definite comes up, then decide."

Something definite did come up. A wealthy family named Bruin needed a governess for their little girl. Corrie had diplomas in child care, needlework, and other domestic skills from normal school. Her moment had finally come.

She told Mama and Papa about the opportunity.

Mama saw immediately what was bothering her. "Don't feel you have to stay at home. We did not ask your brother Willem or your sisters to stay at home."

"Everyone expects the son to leave home. And Nollie and Betsie are still here at home," argued Corrie.

"Nollie teaches school. She doesn't really stay at home."

"But Betsie really stays at home," argued Corrie.

Mama said, "Betsie stays by her own wish."

"But she helps Papa in the shop. You and Aunt Anna need help in the house."

"IF GOD THINKS IT'S A BAD IDEA, YOU'LL KNOW."

Papa said, "You go take that job. If God thinks it's a bad idea, you'll know."

"Couldn't God tell me before I go?"

Papa and Mama laughed.

So Corrie left for Zandvoort, a sunny town by the North Sea, only five miles southwest of Haarlem. Zandvoort had wide sandy beaches and bright sprawling mansions. The Bruins lived in a mansion. The little girl was a difficult charge, but Corrie knew how to hold a child's interest with a good story. Although she soon won the little girl's respect and trust, the Bruin family was very alien to Corrie. They were selfish and cynical. They gloated over their social superiority. They talked of nothing but money and possessions. Corrie had not visited wealthy homes before, as Papa had. She didn't know if wealth caused people to behave this way or if it was just the Bruins, fallen far away from God and the Bible.

Just how far they had fallen was proved when the master of the house confronted her in the bedroom wing of the mansion. He tried to force his affections on Corrie. She ran to her own bedroom and locked the door, still smelling his whisky breath, still hearing his snaky voice.

"Now I know why Aunt Bep is probably like she is," said Corrie to God more than herself. "Who could endure thirty-five years of this? Mama was right to defend her."

Corrie was miserable. She didn't want to stay. How could she remain in such a sinful place? But she didn't want to quit either. Perhaps she could sow the seed of the gospel in the little girl. Who would save this little girl if she left?

"Please Lord, let me know what to do," she prayed.

One day Willem appeared at the mansion. "Aunt Bep is dead. At last her suffering is over. You must come home, Corrie. Aunt Anna is exhausted from caring for her. Mama is getting sicker everyday. Betsie must work in the shop. Nollie has a permanent job as a schoolteacher. And you know Aunt Jans is just Aunt Jans."

The logic escaped Corrie. "Why does Aunt Bep's death change anything? She was no help anyway. It seems as if Aunt Anna would be free to do more housework now."

"Corrie, I have seen the state of the house. Help is needed. None of them would ever complain, you know that."

"I must go home then."

So the decision to leave was made for her. When she left the mansion, she was sad for the little girl. But Corrie knew when the family found out that she had been teaching her about the Bible they would have forced Corrie to go anyway. It was just a matter of time before the child blurted the truth. Surely that was why Corrie was leaving. Why would God let her abandon the child if hope remained? She had to trust God always, but it was painful to leave the child.

The great sandy beach was a novelty for Willem, so they strolled its vastness for a while before they returned to Haarlem.

Slowly, joy grew in her heart. God knew best. But she couldn't bring herself to approve of Willem singing Bach at the top of his lungs.

> "A TRUE CHRISTIAN REJOICES WHEN A LOVED ONE GOES TO HEAVEN TO BE WITH THE LORD."

"How can you sing when Aunt Bep just died?" she asked.

"A true Christian rejoices when a loved one goes to heaven to be with the Lord. Grief is an indulgence for ourselves."

Was Willem right? Couldn't the reason for joy be mistaken for something else? Or was worrying about what other people thought an indulgence, too? Corrie would have to think about it a lot more before she could bring herself to sing. Besides, her grand venture into the world was over, and she felt she had failed.

5.
SEEKING GOD'S KINGDOM

Once again Corrie was home. Willem had been right. Aunt Anna was worn out. Now Corrie was the housekeeper of the home. She didn't get comfort from the acts of cleaning house and cooking like Mama and Aunt Anna did. Her goal every day was simply to finish the work faster than she did the day before.

Mama bluntly told her, "Housework is not fulfilling for you, Corrie."

Papa said, "Yes, Corrie. You need more. What about the new Bible school that just opened in Haarlem?"

So once again Corrie attended school, attacking what seemed to be their entire curriculum at once: ethics, dogmatics, church history, Old Testament, New Testament, Old Testament history, and New Testament history. She studied very hard in her moments outside of housework.

Other activities began to occupy her outside the home, too. Jan Willem Gunning was organizing groups in Holland for foreign missions. All four young ten Booms became active: Corrie, Willem, Nollie, and Betsie. The purpose was to have the Dutch meet real missionaries from around the world and be inspired to support mission work.

During the summer, the groups often met in a wooded area in

the midst of the heather. Corrie's mischief emerged once again. At one conference they had no free time to spend with boys—except before breakfast. So Corrie let it be known she tied a string to her toe and dangled the end of the string outside her window. Soon after her toe felt a gentle tug, Corrie intended to be walking with her catch in the heather.

Corrie went to one conference alone. She heard the testimony of a young missionary named Sadhu Sundar Singh. He told the conference, "As a boy in India, I learned to hate Jesus. I burned a Bible. I threw mud at missionaries. But it was out of frustration, not hate." He prayed that if God really existed, He would reveal Himself. He longed to know if there was life after death, and if there was paradise. He decided the only way to know for sure was to die, so he was going to throw himself in front of a train. Suddenly in a blaze of light he saw a man. The Sadhu heard a voice from the light ask him how long he would deny Him who died for him. Then the Sadhu saw the man's pierced hands.

Corrie was in awe: The Sadhu had had an experience like Paul's on the road to Damascus! How Corrie longed for such an experience. Why was her life so never-endingly drab? Wasn't she, too, a child of God? Didn't she let Jesus come into her heart? And then a very strange thing happened to her. Strolling alone in the heather, she met the Sadhu out walking alone, too. Somehow she never imagined him being alone.

She couldn't contain herself. "Why haven't I had such an experience? I received Jesus as my Savior. I believe in Him with all my heart."

"Then your experience is more

> CORRIE WAS IN AWE: THE SADHU HAD HAD AN EXPERIENCE LIKE PAUL'S ON THE ROAD TO DAMASCUS!

miraculous than mine. In chapter twenty of the book of John, Jesus told Thomas: 'Because thou hast seen me, thou hast believed: blessed are they that have not seen, and yet have believed.' You believe in Him without seeing Him."

Corrie was stunned. Of course the Sadhu was right. Why was she such a doubter, asking for miracles like the Pharisees?

It wasn't much later, back in Haarlem, that Papa was breathless with excitement—and Papa was rarely breathless. One of the greatest moments in the history of Haarlem was imminent. How lucky they were that the great event would not be in the concert hall. It was going to be at Saint Bavo's. And how lucky they were that Uncle Arnold was an usher at Saint Bavo's. The entire ten Boom entourage went in the side door of the cathedral. They sat near the front, but far off to the side in one of the pillared corridors on a wooden bench. Their backs rested against cold stone, so Papa wrapped Mama in a blanket to warm her and soften the stone. Corrie could smell the gas lamps that cast a golden glow inside the cathedral.

Suddenly, within a few feet of her, walked the man himself! He was tall and thin, with a disheveled shock of hair and a long droopy mustache. Corrie could tell he cared nothing for clothes or how he looked. That was exactly how she felt most of the time. He bounded up the stairs that would take him to up to the organ loft and the controls of the great organ. No one so great had played the organ since Mozart. Few could even master the sixty-eight stops.

The cathedral exploded with Bach!

The warm smells, the sight of the cathedral, and the sound of Bach brought Corrie closer to heaven. The organist was thirty-seven-year-old Albert Schweitzer, the world authority on Bach as well as the world authority on organ construction. Schweitzer was also a well-known theologian with controversial writings on

Jesus and Paul. On the way home, Willem and Papa argued over who was the greater Renaissance man: Goethe or Schweitzer?

"And why were we so lucky to get him in Haarlem?" asked Nollie, with her usual bluntness.

"He's raising money for a hospital in the African jungle," said Papa.

"Did some people pay to hear him?" asked Corrie.

"A lot," answered Papa. "Don't forget to thank Uncle Arnold for letting us hear him."

"How noble of Mr. Schweitzer to give the doctors money for their work in deepest Africa," said Mama.

"No, Mama," said Willem. "He's going there himself. He just recently became a medical doctor." Willem laughed. "He's one of the most famous men in Europe. He's welcome in any palace. Now everyone thinks he's crazy."

"He's trying to earn his salvation with good works," protested Betsie.

Corrie had to speak. "No! It's just that being in Christ makes you want to do good works. You can't help yourself."

> "BEING IN CHRIST MAKES YOU WANT TO DO GOOD WORKS. YOU CAN'T HELP YOURSELF."

"Exactly," said Papa.

Corrie was thrilled. It seemed that one might make severe sacrifices for Christ. What would she do after she passed Bible school? She had been studying two years. Soon she would take the final exams. And what would she do with her fistful of diplomas? Tackle the world like Albert Schweitzer?

The first part of the examination at Bible school was to give lessons to students and answer their questions. This she did with ease. After all, she had been giving Bible lessons for several years now anyway. She was very able with students.

The second part of the exam was in Saint Bavo's. It was held in a conference room off one of the pillared corridors. Several ministers sat at a massive oak table. Corrie stood in front of a dead fireplace. The warmth from the Schweitzer concert was gone, too. And the fact that she had played under that very table with Dot years before seemed irrelevant. This room in the cathedral was like a tomb. It really seemed God had deserted her.

They began with ethics.

"You studied only the teachings of Mr. Johnson?" asked one of the ministers, not hiding his displeasure.

"He's one of the instructors," she answered lamely. Corrie knew she was in trouble. Was she in the middle of some faculty dispute? Her brain began to curdle. Too late, she realized God had not deserted her but she had deserted God. Why hadn't she asked for His help sooner? Was she so proud of her learning? The subjects rose one by one. All seven. At the end of the day she had a perfect record: she had not passed one subject. She had failed utterly and completely!

At home Betsie said, "You must take the exam again right away."

But Corrie did not do that. The defeat was too stinging. Maybe she had attempted too much. After all, she could still serve the church by teaching catechism to children. She could still prepare people for confirmation. And she could teach Bible lessons in the public schools. She knew she was a good teacher, even a gifted teacher, thanks to all her practice and Betsie. But she was in no hurry to be humiliated again by the ministers—after all her hard work!

Haarlem was not stagnant. A new Frans Hals Museum opened

in the very home for the elderly where Hals died in 1666. The city's collection of masters was moved there from the town hall. Now Corrie and Betsie had to walk far south on Grote Haut Straat to see the paintings. But they didn't mind. The masterpieces were better lit and more accessible. And the town hall was rebuilding its wonderful gothic tower that was torn down in the 1700s. Haarlem was not standing still.

But the times were full of bad news, too. Europe rippled with rumors of war. Rumors threatened to poison the prayer group that Corrie, Betsie, and Papa met with every week. They took the trolley south to the village of Heemstede every Saturday night. Papa continued to pray for the queen and Holland, but some in the meeting objected now. Christians should not support governments. They should be above the fray. They should seek only the Kingdom of God.

EUROPE RIPPLED WITH RUMORS OF WAR.

Papa countered with what Paul said in chapter two of 1 Timothy:

> *I exhort therefore, that, first of all, supplications, prayers, intercessions, and giving of thanks, be made for all men; for kings, and for all that are in authority; that we may lead a quiet and peaceable life in all godliness and honesty. For this is good and acceptable in the sight of God our Saviour.*

The message seemed clear to Corrie. Holland even managed to stay neutral in the war that exploded across Europe in 1914. It was called the "Great War," whose awful trenches threatened to grind up all the young men in France, Germany, and England.

But the prayer group disintegrated anyway. Its members had been meeting every Saturday night for three years!

Bad news flooded their home, too. Mama was sicker than ever. And a new doctor, Jan van Veen, diagnosed Aunt Jans with diabetes, as sure a death sentence as tuberculosis! Aunt Jans had always been preoccupied with death. She had been dismissed as a worrywart by the ten Boom children, but now it had finally happened. The end was inevitable.

Every week Aunt Jans had to have her blood tested for sugar content, which reflected the progress of the disease. Doctor van Veen decided it would save everyone a lot of time and money if Corrie would do the test at home, so he taught Corrie how to do the test and left vials of chemicals and measuring spoons. Corrie dreaded doing that test every Friday. First she fretted over doing the test correctly on their old coal-burning stove. Then she had to give Aunt Jans the results. God forbid that the final liquid in the beaker would ever be black, which meant death was near. Corrie dreaded seeing the naked fear in her aunt's eyes. How Aunt Jans feared death!

The news was not all bad in the house. Once, Doctor van Veen's nurse—and sister—Tine visited Aunt Jans. Willem was home. He was just months away from being ordained a minister. The moment was electric for the two. He and Tine scheduled their marriage for two months after his ordination. Long overdue cheer entered the home. The ten Booms would have their first wedding. Corrie knew it was much more. Karel would be there.

Corrie was now twenty-one, and Karel was twenty-six. They were no longer girl and man but woman and man. Corrie was as attractive as she would ever be. Betsie spent an hour on Corrie's dark blonde hair that morning. Corrie wore a very elegant silk dress that Betsie had made. Karel came to her like a moth to a flame.

Surely at long last. . .

He was attentive. He flattered her. Could anyone doubt his intentions? Corrie could hardly remember Willem and Tine's wedding, she was so shaken. She thought her heart would explode.

But as surely as she soared into the clouds with that event, another event brought her plummeting down. One Friday morning when she tested her aunt's blood, the liquid in the beaker turned black! How could she tell her? It was too terrible. Aunt Jans might be down from her rooms any second asking about her test.

It was Papa who handled it. First he politely asked Corrie if she was sure she did the test right. Then he asked her to take the beaker to Doctor van Veen. Soon Corrie was back. Yes, the doctor said the test was valid. Aunt Jans had three weeks of life left at the most.

"All right," said Papa. "We'll all go up to see her."

Aunt Jans was writing at her table. Her slight exasperation at the interruption become wonder as she realized she had five visitors: Papa, Mama, Aunt Anna, Betsie, and Corrie. It was Corrie her eyes froze on.

"Today is Friday!" she cried. "Black. . ."

Aunt Jans swept the papers aside. "All is vanity!" She crumpled and sobbed. But abruptly she looked up, tears streaming down her face. "Dear Jesus, I thank You that we must come to You with empty hands. I thank You that You have done everything for us on the cross, and that all we need in life or death is to be sure of this." After her many years of worry about death she triumphed in a twinkling. It was just as Papa had told Corrie all her life. When the time comes, God

> IT WAS JUST AS PAPA HAD TOLD CORRIE ALL HER LIFE. WHEN THE TIME COMES, GOD PROVIDES.

provides for the faithful.

Four months after Aunt Jans's funeral, Willem gave his first sermon. After serving as assistant pastor for almost one year in Uithuizen, a village about as far north as one can go in Holland without walking into the North Sea, Willem was given a church as full pastor in the even smaller village of Made, which was at the southern end of Holland.

No family would miss a minister's first sermon. The ten Booms and Aunt Anna arrived in Made on the train. Three days later, Corrie's wish came true. Karel arrived. He was an assistant pastor himself. He was as free now to marry as Willem had been, a fact that was emblazoned in Corrie's mind.

Karel wasted no time. Soon he and Corrie were walking farther from Willem's rectory each day. The talk was suited to Corrie's fondest dreams. They spoke of what they would do to decorate a rectory, what furniture they would have, a hundred other things.

Their tastes were very much the same. Any differences were trivial. Karel wanted four children; Corrie wanted six. They never actually spoke of marriage but who could doubt that matrimony was in the offing?

Willem doubted, and he let Corrie know it. "I went to school with him for many years, Corrie. I know how he thinks. I know how his family thinks. He must marry well. Even my sister is not good enough for him."

"What a terrible thing to say about your friend."

"He's just a man. Flawed, as we all are."

Gloomy old, hard-nosed Willem, fumed Corrie to herself. How she resented his pessimism sometimes. How she wanted not to listen to him. So she refused to believe. A veteran of hundreds of romance stories, Corrie would never quit now. Karel's stuffy family was a mere obstacle in the plot that just made the resolution—their happy marriage—more satisfying.

And as if to prove how wrong Willem was, Karel and Corrie wrote each other letters. Corrie never relented in her happy barrage of letters but Karel's output declined. He had a good reason, of course. He had become the full pastor at his church. He surely would have written more if he had not taken on so much more responsibility. Visits with parishioners were time-consuming.

One November day Corrie answered a knock on the door to the alley.

"Karel!" she cried.

"Hello, Corrie. I came to introduce my fiancée."

6.
"GIVE YOUR LOVE TO GOD"

"Fiancée!" The word burst from Corrie, a cry of pain. Beside Karel's shoulder was a radiant face above an elegant ermine coat collar. Karel was going to marry well. "Come in," said Corrie numbly.

Karel stayed only a short time to proudly introduce his fiancee to the rest of the family. After they left, Corrie slipped away to her bedroom.

Papa followed her. "Love is the strongest force in the world," he said. "And when it is blocked there is great pain."

"It's excruciating."

"We can kill the love to make it stop hurting. Or we can direct the love to another route."

"I will never love another man. I know that for sure."

"Give your love to God."

After Papa left her, Corrie prayed that her love would go to God. She was only twenty-three years old. Her unmarried status was hardly glaring. Betsie was thirty and unmarried, and Nollie was twenty-five and still single. Corrie had had two aunts who never married at all. She could not feel sorry for herself very long.

She began studying her Bible school subjects again and tried to fine-tune her housework like a virtuoso. After all, housework seemed to be her life's calling. She would set out meat, vegetables, potatoes, and fruit before breakfast. She boiled them then took them off the stove. She wrapped each pot in sixteen pages of newspaper then a towel. This was a slow-cooking method that sealed in the flavors.

She still gave Bible lessons at the public school. And she used her earnings to improve the home. It was Corrie who paid for two toilets that actually flushed the waste into the sewer system. Before that, city workers had to come and empty the waste. It was Corrie who bought a bathtub for the home. Before that, they sponged themselves out of small wash basins.

"What luxury we have now!" praised Mama.

Good news or bad, nothing remained the same very long in the ten Boom house. Mama had a stroke so severe she went into a coma. For two months around the clock they watched her in shifts: Corrie, Betsie, Anna, Papa, and Nollie. And one morning Mama woke up!

They moved her bed into Aunt Jans's front room, so Mama could watch the Haarlemites she loved so much walk on Barteljorisstraat. She recovered enough to walk again but only with help. She could not use her hands to write or knit. She spoke only three words: "Corrie," "yes," and "no." Corrie believed her name was one of the words only because she was with Mama in the kitchen when she had her stroke.

To understand Mama's wishes, they played a guessing game. Mama would answer "yes" or "no" to question after question until the answer she wanted finally came. It was just one more example of the love and patience in the ten Boom home.

The Great War ended. Much of Europe was devastated. Papa was not interested in assigning guilt. He knew many children were destitute. As chairman of the international watchmakers, he urged his membership to take children who had been victims of the war into their homes. The ten Boom house itself had little money but much love.

It wasn't long before the ten Booms welcomed Willy and Katy, urchins from the streets of Germany. Soon they were joined by Ruth and Martha, sisters from Germany. So there were four children ranging in age from ten to four in the home. The children adapted well. Even Mama was up and about, fussing over the newcomers.

> **THE TEN BOOM HOUSE HAD LITTLE MONEY BUT MUCH LOVE.**

The next months were blessed for the ten Booms. The four foster children became so healthy again, they returned to relatives in Germany. Corrie took the exam at the Bible school and passed. And Nollie met another teacher named Flip van Woerden and they were married. At the end of the wedding ceremony, they sang Mama's favorite hymn: "Fairest Lord Jesus."

Corrie was stunned to hear a hoarse voice singing:

> *Fairest Lord Jesus! Ruler of all nature!*
> *O, Thou of God and man the Son!*
> *Thee will I cherish, Thee I will honor,*
> *Thou my soul's glory, joy and crown!*

Was Mama singing? Corrie was afraid to look and break the spell. She peeked. Yes!

Mama sang verse after verse, finishing:

> *Beautiful Savior! Lord of the nations!*
> *Son of God and Son of Man!*
> *Glory and honor, praise, adoration*
> *Now and forevermore be Thine!*

It seemed a miracle. Was Mama recovering?

No, she relapsed into her three words, and within a month she passed away. Corrie remembered her singing in the church as an even greater miracle. No bland medical explanation would ever satisfy her. Yet Corrie wrestled with the injustice of Mama's suffering. Why did such a warm, loving woman have to suffer like she had? Why? Finally she decided that she had learned from Mama that love could transcend all human affliction. Her whole life, Mama had shown her love by doing things for people, but in the end, with her normal expressions of love paralyzed, Mama's love still radiated, whole and complete. Nothing can defeat love.

Christmas time that year was a great turning point for Corrie. She was twenty-eight years old. The change started innocently enough. Betsie got the flu, so Corrie helped Papa in the shop. She greeted customers and worked with the bills and correspondence. As Betsie got better, she began picking up Corrie's duties in the house. Sensitive, artistic Betsie was much better at housework than Corrie. She had a special touch, like Aunt Anna. It was painfully obvious to Corrie.

But the reverse was true, too. Corrie was much better at working in the shop than Betsie had been. God surely arranged this insight. And to make it a source of joy and not consternation, they each loved their new role. Without a moment's hesitation, they exchanged duties.

Corrie was amazed at Papa. He had trained under Howu, recognized as one of the great clockmakers. He published a newspaper for watchmakers. He was chairman of the international watchmakers. He was known far and wide as the best watchmaker in Holland.

But he was so inept at sound business principles she was flabbergasted. He had no bookkeeping system. He forgot to make out bills. He did not price his watches low enough to sell. He closed his shop just as people began to stroll the street after they got off work and window-shop. He didn't even light up his windows in the evening. He shuttered them!

The truth was, Papa cared nothing for money.

Corrie witnessed an example of Papa's attitude about money one day as she was setting up a book-keeping system in a set of new ledgers she bought. An obviously wealthy customer came in the shop and picked out a very expensive watch. In an offhand way, he complained about his old watch, "I bought this watch from old Van Houten. It doesn't keep good time. I took it back three times."

> THE TRUTH WAS, PAPA CARED NOTHING FOR MONEY.

Papa perked up. "Mr. Van Houten died. His son runs the shop now. Let me see your watch, sir."

"Here is the lemon," said the man, slightly aggravated.

Papa opened the back of the watch. "Here's the problem." He made an adjustment with a tiny tool. He handed it back to the man. "It's as good as new. You don't need a new watch."

"But are you sure?"

"Yes. And please go back to Van Houten's son. He's a very good watchmaker. He's distracted because he's mourning. It's not easy losing a father."

After the man left, Corrie approached. "Papa, was that good business?"

Papa looked at her with disappointment. "I spoke the gospel at Van Houten's funeral."

There was nothing she could say. Papa was right. He truly lived in Christ.

Keeping the books and welcoming customers was not enough

for Corrie. As soon as she established a system she was happy with, she asked Papa if she could work on watches.

"You're the only one of the children who ever asked me that," he answered in surprise. "But if you had been the fourth I would still say, 'Yes, of course you may.' I will teach you."

So Corrie was trained by the best watchmaker in Holland. Papa even sent her to Switzerland to work in a watch factory for a while, but soon she was back. With Papa's help, she became the first woman watchmaker licensed in Holland. Her specialty was the new rage: wristwatches. Even that was not enough for Corrie. She gave Bible lessons to children as always, but now she had a special class for the disabled. She was sure Jesus revealed himself to these children.

> CORRIE BECAME THE FIRST WOMAN WATCHMAKER LICENSED IN HOLLAND.

Once Corrie asked her class, "How are a prophet and a priest the same?"

A girl answered, "They both take messages between God and men."

"And how are they different?"

The girl answered, "A prophet stands with his back to God and talks to the people. A priest stands with his back to the people and talks to God."

Another time Corrie was telling the story of Jesus feeding the five thousand and a boy jumped up to yell, "There is plenty for everyone! Take as much as you like!" The boy was thrilled by the miracle.

In other ways the children were disabled, but Corrie had no doubt at all that the gospel reached the children with the help of the Holy Spirit.

Encouraged by a wealthy ladies' club concerned about lack of activities for teenaged girls in Haarlem, Corrie and Betsie started taking a few girls for walks before church on Sunday. They ran a blunt ad in the newspaper:

> Do You Like To Go on Walks?
> If You Want to Meet Other Girls and Have Fun,
> Come to the ten Boom Shop at
> Barteljorisstraat 19.

It seemed like a small thing. But soon they and the girls were meeting on Wednesdays to walk to gardens in the wealthy suburb of Bloemendaal near the seashore. Estate owners were happy to encourage exercise for young girls. When the weather got cold, Corrie and Betsie began meeting with the girls in large rooms in wealthy homes in the same suburbs. The meat of such endeavors—the gospel—was always sandwiched in the middle of fun things to do.

Corrie's club work grew into something she never imagined in the beginning. Early in the effort, she and Betsie had to recruit other young ladies to help. Soon they had forty ladies, each with a troop of eight girls. Their three hundred girls became quite a presence in Haarlem. Once a year, they rented the concert hall to show a thousand friends and relatives the skills they were learning in the clubs. Corrie was a fearless public speaker by now. Always, right in the middle of the show, she offered the gospel in talks with catchy titles like "God's telephone is never busy," or "Do you have your radio tuned to the right station?" Her organization officially became the Haarlem Girls' Clubs. Soon they were welcomed into the Christian Union of the Lady Friends of the Young Girl, with headquarters in Switzerland. The ladies and the girls now wore uniforms!

Another death struck the family. Faithful Aunt Anna died. All four Luitingh sisters were now dead. Every one had died in the ten Boom house within a span of one decade. It was as if they were a certain kind of fine clock all wound by God at the same time about seventy years before.

Papa's house had once resounded with nine people living in seven bedrooms. Now only Papa, Betsie, and Corrie remained. Papa was not one to waste empty bedrooms. The ten Booms had bedrooms to share. And plenty of love.

Papa said, "Do you remember what Mama said about missionaries?"

"Of course," said Corrie. "Her own mother—my dear Grandma Luitingh—lost both missionary parents on the same day in Indonesia. She was just a small child, an orphan in a strange land."

Betsie added, "I remember Mama saying if we did anything to help the missionary effort we should help the children of missionaries."

"When do we begin?" asked Corrie.

They began to take in children left in Holland by missionaries. This was no small undertaking. These were children to be raised to adulthood. And even though they were the offspring of missionaries and usually eager to please, many were at a difficult age.

THEY BEGAN TO TAKE IN CHILDREN LEFT IN HOLLAND BY MISSIONARIES. THESE WERE CHILDREN TO BE RAISED TO ADULTHOOD.

The first ones to arrive were eleven- and twelve-year-old sisters Puck and Hans, and their brother Hardy, fourteen. Soon a girl named Lessie arrived. And not long after that, Miep and another girl came to live with the ten Booms. The new children named the house *Beje*, pronounced "bay-yay," the initials of Bartel Joris, for whom Barteljorisstraat was named. Betsie and Corrie became their "aunts." Papa became *Opa*, Dutch for "grandpa".

Once, before the Bible reading at supper, Puck said, "Opa, let's read Psalm 117 tonight. I really like that one," trying not to smile. Psalm 117 had only twenty-nine words.

"Psalm 117?" answered Opa agreeably as he turned the pages. "Oh," he said innocently, "let's read 119 instead." Psalm 119 had 176 verses and 2,337 words! Hardy counted them later and reminded Puck of those facts for a very long time. So the children learned gentle Opa was no fool, and the Bible was to be taken seriously.

A watch company sent Papa complimentary red caps, and soon Corrie was exercising the six children on long walks. People in Haarlem joked about Corrie's "Red Cap Club." They shook their heads in amazement. Wasn't this the same woman organizing all the teenage girls in Haarlem? The answer was yes. Corrie was really devoted to young people. God's love gave her love to give.

A sense of humor helped, too. Her club girls had a gymnasium section. At one of the meetings they voted on a slogan. Corrie always knew she was high-hipped with pigeon toes, but now shorts revealed another flaw: knock-knees. One girl looking at Corrie's legs suggested the slogan: *We make straight what is crooked!* Corrie did not mind. She loved to be teased. To her, teasing was a form of friendship. She was not too proud to take a joke, even though young people often pushed her to the limit.

Summers became a time for camping out. The first rule of camp was not to gossip. Instead the highlight of each day were inspiring stories around the campfire. Eventually Corrie got the use of a cabin that would hold sixty girls. On the last evening of their campout, she would sneak from the cabin after lights-out and sing a warm good-bye song. But one year her song was drowned out by a horrible din. She was sure she battled the devil himself. She didn't stop singing. She fought the good fight. The next day her girls insisted that she had never sung more beautifully and that they didn't hear any noise at all.

Dealing with her leaders took patience, too. One leader was so exasperating she was a legend. She was nicknamed *Kipslang,* Dutch for "chicken-snake," because she told her girls the snake in the Garden of Eden had legs like a chicken. One of her meetings broke up with girls throwing chairs at each other. Corrie counted ten clubs that had formed from girls who were first attracted to Kipslang's outrageous group then fled it! Corrie was too kind to ask any leader to quit, so Kipslang stayed.

Separate clubs were formed for individual activities, too. Corrie's favorite was her Catechism club. This was the one in which girls studied to enter the Dutch Reformed Church. But Corrie taught the gospel in small potent doses in all groups. One girl who accepted Jesus was Pietje, a small hunchback. One day Corrie was told to rush to the hospital.

> CORRIE'S FAVORITE WAS HER CATECHISM CLUB, IN WHICH GIRLS STUDIED TO ENTER THE DUTCH REFORMED CHURCH.

Little Pietje was dying, her face twisted in pain. Corrie said, "It's such a comfort to know Jesus is our judge. How He loves you, Pietje!"

Pietje's face relaxed. Corrie stroked her forehead and prayed aloud for the Good Shepherd to take His lamb into His arms and carry her through the valley of the shadow of death to His Father's house with many mansions. As Corrie said, "Amen," Pietje opened her eyes and smiled. Then she died.

After many years of blessed health in the Beje, Papa ten Boom was struck down by hepatitis. It was 1930. He was within days of reaching his three score and ten years of life. His beard turned white as snow as he clung to life in small, inconspicuous Saint Elizabeth's hospital. What would Corrie and Betsie do without Papa?

Corrie prayed that God's will be done.

7.
THE OCCUPATION

Papa ten Boom recovered. Upon his return to the Beje, he was visited by a committee of shopkeepers, a bargeman, and all those Haarlemites who dropped into his shop for his ever dependable friendly conversation. They gave him the latest invention: a radio, a table model with a speaker on top like a giant morning glory.

"What joy it will bring the ten Booms, as much as we love music," said Papa in thanks.

Papa's illness was a wake-up call for Corrie. He was seventy years old. They had already hired a bookkeeper for the shop, a surly woman named Toos, who seemed to like no one in the world except Papa. But, unfriendly as she was, Toos really helped Corrie more than she helped Papa. It was time to get Papa some help.

One day, in walked a shabby man who introduced himself as Christoffels. "I am looking for work," he added.

After only a moment or two, Papa hired him. Papa was excited later. "Don't judge him by his ragged clothing. He's the old style clock man, the kind who roams the country fixing any kind of watch or clock you can name. He will be invaluable to us."

Corrie's girls' club evolved into the Girl Guides, another international organization. This relieved her of many duties. But Corrie became unhappy with the Girl Guides. They seemed to pander more and more to short-sighted squawkers in the organization who tried to squelch the teaching of Christianity. Memories of Pietje and many other girls who had died, saved in Jesus because of the club, made it impossible for Corrie to remain in such an organization. So she left it—with all her girls.

Her group of girls became local again: the Triangle Club. The triangle represented social, intellectual, and physical skills. But the triangle was inside a circle. This meant being in the right relationship with God. Their four club rules were:

1. Seek your strength through prayer.
2. Be open and trustworthy.
3. Bear your difficulties cheerfully.
4. Develop the gifts that God gave you.

Corrie openly embraced Christianity—but as always wisely gave the gospel in small, potent doses.

In 1937 the watch shop celebrated its first one hundred years. Christoffels and Toos were there even earlier that morning. Nollie was to come later with her husband Flip and their six children. Willem and Tine would be there with their four. And the ten Booms expected many visitors that day. Papa was seventy-seven now, the Opa for many in Haarlem.

It was a golden age for the three ten Booms at Beje. Troubles seemed in the distant past. Dear Aunt Anna, the last sister, had died over twelve years ago. Such peace, such prosperity, such health worried Corrie a little. And there was that evil which appeared on the eastern horizon. Since 1927, when

> WHEN WILLEM STUDIED IN GERMANY, HE RAILED ABOUT WHAT WAS HAPPENING.

Willem studied in Germany for his doctorate, he had railed about what was happening in Germany. Something very insidious was occurring in the universities, said gloomy Willem. The same horrible thing was happening among the mayors of the towns. The thing growing in Germany was a socialism of the most heartless kind. It called itself the National Socialist German Workers and became known as the Nazi party. The poor, the old, the feebleminded, the handicapped were enemies of progress. Soon Jews were included as enemies, too, then Communists.

The Nazi outrage was engineered by a man named Hitler. He appeared laughable at first—comical then maddening. But soon there was nothing amusing about him at all. Holland would stay neutral no matter what happened, reasoned Corrie. And surely gloomy Willem was exaggerating about the Nazis. But sometimes she wondered if she had not quite forgiven him for predicting what Karel would do.

The day of the hundredth anniversary, people rapped on the door to the alley constantly. Flowers, flowers, and more flowers arrived. And Christoffels, of all people, decorous in coat and tie as he had never been before, was greeting well-wishers and formally escorting them into the shop like a butler at a mansion. Everyone seemed almost saintly today. It was going to be a great day for Papa.

The Beje was soon milling with visitors. One of Corrie's favorites was Herman Sluring, a man the ten Boom sisters had dubbed "Pickwick" many years before. To them, he looked just like the Charles Dickens character. He was grossly overweight, and his wideset eyes darted different directions like a chameleon's. Both he and Papa were always engulfed in children. Papa attracted them with the pockets of his suit coat, which buzzed and ticked and whirred because he carried dozens of watches. Pickwick lured them with tricks like balancing a cup of coffee on his mountainous belly.

All day long, guests flowed in and out of the Beje. Papa had hundreds of friends. Willem's family was there, and finally Willem himself came in the late afternoon. In Hilversum, some twenty-five miles east of Haarlem, he ran the Dutch Reformed Church's outreach program for Jews. He even opened a home for destitute Jews, so his Jewish companion should have been no surprise. But he was a surprise. His face was red and raw.

In a bitter voice, Willem explained, "He's from Germany. Hooligans in the street set his beard on fire."

"Oh, that Willem!" complained Corrie to Betsie. "Is it necessary for him to taint Papa's big day with politics?"

But as the months passed, Corrie began to understand. They had two radios in the Beje now. The table model was in Aunt Jans's big room, and they had a small portable radio on the kitchen table, a present from Pickwick. Almost all the time, the speakers carried blissful concerts carefully managed by Betsie from radio schedules, but once in a while as the dial searched for a station, the speaker erupted with fiery screams from Germany. They seemed straight from hell. This man Hitler sounded like the devil himself.

THIS MAN HITLER SOUNDED LIKE THE DEVIL HIMSELF.

Papa's young apprentice, a German named Otto, brought the message home to the Beje loud and clear. One day he attacked Christoffels. His reason was that Christoffels was old, decrepit, and worthless. Papa fired Otto immediately. Later Papa made excuses for him: He was young and confused. Gloomy Willem said no, Otto was a typical German these days.

In 1938 the radio told them that Germany was meeting with

Italy, France, and Britain in Munich to discuss Hitler's demand for an area of Czechoslovakia called the Sudetenland. After the meeting, Hitler's Germany possessed the Sudetenland.

Papa said, "The bully got his first piece of the pie. He will soon be after another."

Surely it wasn't that bad, thought Corrie. Who knew anything about a place called Sudetenland? But six months later Hitler's army walked into Czechoslovakia and took over the entire country. The radio said the American president Franklin Roosevelt wanted an assurance from Hitler that he would not start a fight with certain countries. Roosevelt listed twenty-nine countries.

"There," said Papa, "surely Hitler will listen to a powerful Dutchman like Roosevelt."

But the radio crackled two weeks later with Hitler's answer. It was a long speech, not in the usual screaming style—but humorous, all the while mocking Roosevelt, ridiculing him. Corrie shivered. This man Hitler was afraid of no one. And he was not a raving lunatic. He was diabolically shrewd. Thank God Holland was a neutral country.

Later, in 1939, Germany signed a pact with Russia. "That is very bad," said Papa. "Hitler just made sure the Russians will stay on the sidelines. He will conquer Poland now."

"But why would the Russians do that?" asked Corrie.

"Maybe Hitler will give them part of Poland."

"But can he conquer Poland?" asked Betsie.

"I'm afraid we will find out very soon," answered Papa.

One week later, Germany invaded Poland. This conflict was not like the one in Czechoslovakia. The Poles fought hard. But the news on the radio was heartbreaking. Hitler's tanks crushed horses of the Polish cavalry. The Germans split Poland with Russia. The Americans declared their neutrality. Was Roosevelt afraid to fight, just like Hitler said? The French and British declared war on Germany. Which was worse? To fight or to be neutral? Who could know?

Nothing more happened for weeks. The Russians invaded Finland, but that hardly concerned Holland. Perhaps Hitler was satisfied. Was he telling the truth about his intentions? Perhaps everyone had been too gloomy.

One evening Papa said sadly, "Roosevelt is still warning Germany not to go further. Now he's warning Italy not to join Germany. But is anyone listening to him? Everyone knows by now the Americans are going to stay neutral."

"But Papa," objected Corrie, "don't you want them to stay neutral?"

"This maniac Hitler may not permit any country to stay neutral."

"Even us?" gasped Betsie.

"Even us," said Papa gloomily.

Only the French and British opposed Hitler. The British had a new prime minister, a belligerent man named Churchill. The British were already fighting the Germans at sea. The German battleships *Graf Spee* and *Deutschland* were the rage of the sea. They sank ship after British ship. The battleships were invincible, bragged the Nazis.

But finally the British navy trapped the German battleships in a bay in Argentina. The battleships were destroyed. Corrie felt her heart soar. Then she realized she was caught up in war fever. Oh, war was madness.

In late December of 1939, Hitler said the Jewish-capitalist countries would not survive the twentieth century. Was he only indulging his flaming rhetoric again? Wasn't Holland a capitalist country? Thank God Holland was neutral. Surely Papa was wrong.

Hitler's armies were doing nothing on the European continent now.

But suddenly, in April of 1940, Hitler invaded Norway and Denmark. He said he was protecting them from the French and British who had designs on them. Corrie remembered the summer she and her girls had hiked into Germany to tour the Rhine. It was so easy. Germany was less than one hundred miles away. The Germans had been nice to them. What had happened?

In early May the prime minister of Holland came on the radio to reassure the Dutch: Holland was neutral.

Papa snapped off the volume.

"Papa," objected Betsie, "don't you want to hear him?"

"I'M SORRY FOR ALL THE DUTCH WHO DON'T KNOW GOD. BECAUSE WE WILL BE ATTACKED BY THE GERMANS, AND WE WILL BE DEFEATED."

"I'm sorry for all the Dutch who don't know God. Because we will be attacked by the Germans, and we will be defeated."

It seemed like Papa, who tried to see the good in everything, had sealed their grim fate. Corrie went to bed, and for the first time in her life she prayed her Papa was wrong. Surely this nightmare couldn't be happening. She awoke hours later to lightning and thunder.

"No! That is not a thunderstorm!" she cried.

Other noises popped and boomed and crackled. Men. Men and their machines. She raced down the stairs and checked on Papa. He was asleep. She dashed into Betsie's bedroom. Betsie was sitting up, terrified. They hugged each other.

"Most of the big explosions seem far away to the east," said

Betsie. "I'll bet the Germans are bombing Amsterdam."

War!

It was the worst shock of Corrie's life. She seemed plunged into hell. In the hours that followed, she and Betsie prayed for Holland. Betsie even prayed for the Germans. What sisters Corrie had! Nollie could not tell a lie, and Betsie prayed for everyone, including their enemies.

While praying, Corrie had a vision. Surely she couldn't have dreamed it. Who could have slept at such a time? In the town square she saw four enormous black horses pulling a farm wagon. In the wagon was Corrie herself! And Papa. And Betsie. She realized the wagon was crowded. There was Pickwick and Toos—and Willem and Nollie! Even young nephew Peter. None of them could get off the wagon. They were being taken somewhere. What could the vision mean?

The bombing stopped.

Once again they listened to the radio, joined by Papa, finally looking all of his eighty years. The radio said Germans were bombing airports all over Holland. Germans had parachuted into Rotterdam, Dordrecht, and Moerdijk.

"How odd," said Betsie. "Moerdijk is a tiny village."

Papa said, "No. The Germans want to capture the bridges in those three places, so their tanks can move freely back and forth from northern Holland to southern Holland." Dear Papa, seemingly so naive in business, was so wise in the affairs of men. But how could one read the Bible like he did and not know every nuance of men and their flawed ambitions?

After dawn the Dutch people of Haarlem walked the streets in a daze. The radio had urged them to tape their windows, but there was little else to do. Even Papa strolled the streets. They walked through the town square. They crossed the bridge over the

Spaarne. They walked to the ancient Amsterdam Gate that once sealed the city walls. They visited the great cherry tree called the Bride of Haarlem. There were no craters, no shattered windows, no crumpled bricks.

"All the bombs must have fallen on the Schiphol airport at Amsterdam," observed Corrie, remembering what the radio said.

But there were damaged hearts in Haarlem, especially among the Jews. Fear was written on their faces. This was a bad time for them. They knew what Hitler had been saying about Jews. All anyone could do was wait. The queen fled to Britain on May 13. The Dutch army collapsed into a small area from Amsterdam to Rotterdam they called "Fortress Holland," as if it were impregnable against the Nazis. Within two days the Dutch army surrendered.

Days later German soldiers arrived. They were the eighteenth Army of German Army Group B under General Fedor von Bock. There was no resistance. The Germans marched on parade, goose-stepping in crisp gray-and-black uniforms. They had tanks and cannons, trucks and half-tracks, and hundreds of huge red flags, each with a black swastika inside a white circle. It was ironic that the flags reminded Corrie of her Triangle Club, except the swastika was completely at odds with God, swirling and ripping and tearing like blades of the devil.

The Germans assured the Dutch that they had come to defend them against the French and British, but the news on the radio, of how they ruthlessly bombed Rotterdam while that Dutch city tried to negotiate its terms of surrender, exposed the lie. It seemed to Corrie that the German soldiers were embarrassed to have killed their friends and neighbors, the Dutch. Or was that only her wishful thinking?

The occupation began. The government was now under the control of Reichs Commissioner Artur von Seyss-Inquart.

Holland was now part of the glorious Third Reich, which was to be the third great empire, after the Roman Empire and Charlemagne's Empire.

"They say the Third Reich will last a thousand years!" moaned Betsie.

"No. Such transparent evil cannot last," objected Papa. "But I fear it will last a long time."

At first, the occupation did not seem so evil to Corrie. The German soldiers had money. They bought things at the shop. They even bought all of Papa's *winkeldochters*—"shop daughters"—clocks and watches that had been in the shop for years without being sold. There were a few inconveniences, such as that the Dutch could not be in the street after ten o'clock at night. But what respectable citizen would be out then anyway? Each Dutch citizen had to carry an identity card in a pouch hanging from a "necklace." Food and merchandise had to be purchased with coupons from ration books. Was that so bad? The Germans were very well organized. The Dutch could have no telephones, but heaven knows people listened to too much gossip on phones anyway. The newspapers no longer carried any real news. Any fool realized that. But the news was depressing anyway. All of Europe was falling into the Third Reich, even France.

"This occupation is seductive," said Papa after a few weeks. "The Nazis are more patient than I thought."

When the Dutch were ordered to turn in their radios, they were upset. Radios were still novel. They loved to listen to their

HOLLAND WAS NOW PART OF THE GLORIOUS THIRD REICH, TO BE THE THIRD GREAT EMPIRE, AFTER THE ROMAN EMPIRE AND CHARLEMAGNE'S EMPIRE.

concerts. Willem insisted the Dutch would also soon be hopelessly lost in a world of never-ending lies and deceit. Even Nollie's sixteen-year-old son Peter knew it. So Corrie was convinced to turn in the portable radio and lie to the German officer about not owning another one. She felt bad about lying. She told herself she was only being as wise and shrewd as a snake but innocent as a dove, as Jesus advised one to be against a world of evil. But she didn't seek the opinion of Betsie or Papa.

CORRIE WAS CONVINCED TO TURN IN THE PORTABLE RADIO AND LIE ABOUT NOT OWNING ANOTHER ONE.

Betsie said, "Oh, did the Nazis let us keep our other radio?" But she had nothing to add when she realized Peter was hiding their table radio under the staircase.

The Dutch were not pleased about losing their bicycles either. Everyone rode bicycles, even Corrie. It started with German soldiers stopping riders and confiscating the tires. The tires were shipped back to Germany. Rubber was precious. The practical Dutch could understand that, even if they didn't like it. They quickly learned to wrap the rims with cloth and ride the bicycles anyway. But soon the soldiers were confiscating the bicycles. So the Nazis had more in mind. They didn't want the Dutch moving around. Soon the Dutch hid thousands of bicycles inside their homes.

Corrie had to surrender her work with her girls' clubs. The Nazis were not about to allow any well-organized network of over three hundred Dutch to exist in one town—even teenaged girls and their leaders. Who knew how such people might be used by an underground of traitors to the Third Reich? Gradually the ten o'clock curfew was moved earlier and earlier. It wasn't long into the

Nazi occupation until being out after dark was forbidden. Nighttime was just too convenient for Dutch troublemakers to move around.

"The nighttime is good for us now," said Kik, Willem's oldest son. And his sentiments were echoed by Peter. Corrie noticed that young men and older boys seemed very active at night. What kind of mischief were they up to?

To Corrie, the Nazis were no more than a dreadful nuisance, almost like parents who were far too strict. So a letter from the ten Booms' foster child, Hans, shocked her.

8.
HIDING JEWS

This is horrible," cried Corrie as she read the letter from Hans.

Hans lived in Rotterdam with her husband and two small children. The German soldiers there bragged that the terrible bombing of Rotterdam was a brilliant tactic of war called *schrecklichkeit*.

The deaths of eight hundred Dutchmen were not necessary to capture Rotterdam; the deaths were designed to fill the Dutch with such fear that their resistance would permanently vanish. Hans and her family now lived in a cellar in constant fear. Hans was pregnant again, too.

SIGNS APPEARED IN DUTCH SHOPS: NO JEWS SERVED HERE.

"Sweet little Hans. Who can love such people as these horrid Nazis?" Corrie pointedly asked Betsie and Papa.

"Didn't Jesus with His last breath on the cross forgive His tormentors?" countered Papa.

Never was Corrie torn by so much doubt. Who could love Nazis? They were such snakes. They even turned on the Russians in June of 1941 and were mangling Russian troops on a battle front east of Germany. The Nazis seemed invincible. Their occupation of western Europe displayed more evil every day. Signs appeared in

Dutch shops: No JEWS SERVED HERE. Surely those were just a few misguided anti-Semites, said Papa. But then a sign appeared in a public park: No JEWS ALLOWED. Soon Jews were made to wear a large yellow star of David with *Jood*, the Dutch word for Jew, sewed inside.

Papa was dismayed. "The Jews are the apples of God's eye. The Germans cannot go further than this. I pity them."

Watches left for repair in the shop began to accumulate. The owners seemed not to want to pick them up. Most of the neglected watches belonged to Jews. Were they afraid to come to get them? Papa would have his shop boy jump on his bicycle and deliver them.

The shop boy kept coming back.

"Is no one at home at the Levines?" asked Papa.

"I asked their neighbors," explained the boy, not wanting to realize the horror of what he knew. "The neighbors said the Gestapo took the Levines for questioning. No one has seen them in weeks." The Dutch heard more and more rumors about the Gestapo. They were the secret police, supposedly the very worst of the Nazis.

Then Mr. Kan's watch shop closed. Mr. Kan and his wife were nowhere to be seen. Papa was stunned. Mr. Kan had been there in downtown Haarlem for thirty-one years. He was a good businessman, much better than Papa. He wouldn't just leave suddenly.

"Where have Mr. Kan and his wife gone?" asked Papa of anyone who would listen.

The question was never answered.

British broadcasts on the radio kept saying German planes used Dutch airports now to fly missions over England and drop bombs.

"Dutch airports?" asked Papa. "It can't be true, or the English would be bombing us."

But more and more they heard the roar of engines overhead at night. Was it because Haarlem was below the path of German planes flying from the airport at Amsterdam to England? One night in the summer, the sky over Haarlem not only roared and whined with the noise of engines but flickered with light. The fiery traces were not the paths of shooting stars but bullets! There was a battle above Haarlem. The ten Booms huddled in the dining room until the night sky was silent.

Later Corrie found a hunk of metal on her bed. "Betsie! If I had been in bed it would have struck me right in the head."

Betsie smiled patiently. "In God's world there are no 'ifs.' No place is any safer than any other place. Our only safety is in the center of God's will. Let us pray that we know His will."

For a year and a half, the three ten Booms had tried to live their normal lives. One November morning in 1941 changed that. Corrie was on the sidewalk folding back the shutters on the watch shop when four German soldiers with rifles rushed into the furrier's shop across the street from the Beje. Moments later a soldier prodded the owner, Mr. Weil, into the street with a rifle muzzle.

> FOUR GERMAN SOLDIERS WITH RIFLES RUSHED INTO THE FURRIER'S SHOP ACROSS THE STREET FROM THE BEJE.

Corrie ran inside the Beje. She and Betsie watched through their shop window in horror as the soldiers smashed up Mr. Weil's shop and stole his furs. One soldier opened a second-story window. Clothing cascaded to the sidewalk. Mr. Weil stood on the sidewalk in a daze.

"We must help Mr. Weil," cried Corrie.

She and Betsie ran out to help him gather his clothing off the sidewalk then quickly they ushered him down the alley and up into their dining room.

"Mr. Weil!" exclaimed Papa happily, not realizing what happened. He cherished visitors.

"I must warn my wife," worried Mr. Weil. "She's visiting relatives in Amsterdam. She must not come home."

Corrie felt herself pulled into the battle. "Willem will know what to do." And almost as if in a dream she found herself walking north on Kruisstraat to the railway station then riding the train through Amsterdam all the way to Hilversum. She got off the train at midday.

Tine was at Willem's nursing home with her grown son Kik. They listened to Corrie. Kik said, "Have Mr. Weil ready to go as soon as it gets dark. And what is the Amsterdam address where Mrs. Weil is visiting?" He sighed, as if reluctant to draw his fifty-year-old Aunt Corrie into the fray.

Once again Corrie rode the train between Hilversum and Haarlem. That night Kik came for Mr. Weil and they disappeared into the dark alley.

When Corrie saw him two weeks later, she whispered, "How are the Weils?"

"If you are going to work in the underground, you must not ask questions. The less you know, the less the Gestapo can torture out of you." Kik was smiling apologetically, but Corrie shivered. Everyone in Holland now feared the Gestapo.

The significance of Kik's words slowly sank in. Her nephew Kik was involved with the underground. And surely so was her brother Willem. Who else?

Some of the Dutch openly defied the Nazis, and once again it hit home at the Beje. This time it was Peter, Nollie's son. He played the organ at the church in Velsen, north of Haarlem. Occasionally Corrie went to their service with Papa and Betsie, so they could hear him play. On May 12, 1942, after the sermon and hymns and the final prayer, the organ began blasting nothing other than *Wilhelmus*!

"Oh, Peter," groaned Corrie. "Such defiance."

The Nazis had banned the Dutch national anthem *Wilhelmus*. And as Corrie and her family went to Nollie's house in south Haarlem for lunch, the magnitude of Peter's indiscretion mounted for Corrie. Nollie and Flip were sheltering two Jews: a young blonde woman named Annaliese, who looked very Dutch and went about freely, and Katrien, an older woman who posed as their maid. What would happen to this house if the Gestapo came after Peter? Would his proud moment of defiance cost two Jews their freedom? And who else would be lost?

Wednesday morning it happened. The Gestapo arrested Peter. They were myopic. They overlooked the two Jewish women. It was not until Saturday that Nollie and Flip heard Peter was in a federal prison in Amsterdam.

It seemed to Corrie that the ten Booms and their whole extended family were irretrievably committed to defying the Nazis. Would word of their defiance spread? It was not two weeks later that Corrie heard a desperate knock on the alley door.

Corrie didn't hesitate a moment when she saw the fear in the woman's eyes. "Come inside!" She rushed the woman up to the dining room.

"I'm Mrs. Kleermacher. I'm a Jew," said the woman.

"GOD'S PEOPLE ARE ALWAYS WELCOME IN THIS HOUSE," SAID PAPA.

"God's people are always welcome in this house," said Papa.

"Thank God," she said. "I heard you ten Booms helped Mr. Weil."

The Gestapo had ordered her to close her family clothing store. Her husband had already been arrested. What choice did she have now but to hide? And what choice did the three ten Booms have but to hide her?

Two nights later, an elderly Jewish couple joined Mrs. Kleermacher in hiding. Corrie knew the situation was explosive. Jews were fleeing to the Beje. It could be nothing more than a rest stop. The Jews had to move on to safer places. But where did they go? Once again she traveled to Hilversum on the train.

This time Willem was there. He said, "Most Jews work on farms. But that's getting more and more difficult. Even the farms must account for their food now. We can find places on farms if they bring food ration books with them. Otherwise—"

"But Jews aren't issued ration books!" cried Corrie.

"They can't be counterfeited either. The Nazis change the design too often."

"But what can we do, Willem?"

"We must steal the ration books." And he sighed as he noticed Corrie waiting expectantly. "I can't do it, Corrie. They watch me now every moment."

And Corrie remembered someone. "I know a man named—"

Willem gently put a finger on her lips. "Don't tell me his name, dear sister."

She fretted about it all the way home on the train. There was a girl who had come to her Sunday school class for the disabled for twenty years. Her father worked at the Food Office. Could Corrie prevail on this man for help? She had sought help from people for years for her many projects, but never was so much at stake as now.

What would the Gestapo do to this man if he were caught? What if he were a Nazi sympathizer? What would happen to her and Betsie and Papa? Never had the world seemed so evil. And why was she doing this at her age?

"Oh, please God, help me," she prayed.

She rode her bicycle to the man's house that very night. He listened to her impassively. There was no anger, no sympathy. Perhaps she saw some fear.

He sighed. "The ration books must be accounted for a dozen ways. There is only one way to get any books for your purposes."

"Yes?" she asked hopefully.

"We must be robbed. It happens more and more these days with Dutch people so desperate for food. They wouldn't necessarily suspect me. How many books do you want?"

Three? No, she argued with herself, there would be other Jews fleeing. Five? How many should she ask for? He was going to be robbed. He would be grilled by the Gestapo. That sacrifice should not come cheap. "I need one hundred ration books," she said stoutly, hardly believing her own ears.

A week later she visited the man again. The food ration books were in an envelope. His face was hamburger. His friends had done it to him. He paid a heavy price for the books. Yet she knew the Gestapo probably would not have believed anything less than a bloody thrashing.

"I NEED ONE HUNDRED RATION BOOKS," SHE SAID, HARDLY BELIEVING HER OWN EARS.

"God will bless you for this," she said.

The glory of it was that the staged robbery did not have to be repeated. The last coupon in the book was presented to the Food Office for the next month's ration book. So Corrie had one hundred permanent food rations to dispense. One hundred lives saved!

But it was much too dangerous for Corrie to come to the Food Office. Sometimes the shrewdest of the Gestapo were lurking there. Her brave helper preferred to bring them to the Beje. He was once a meterman for the electric company and soon they worked out a plan where he would come every month in his meterman's uniform to check their meter. The quick precious exchange would take place then.

One night Kik surprised Corrie and took her out into the darkness of the night to Aerdenhout, a wealthy suburb of Haarlem. Inside a mansion milled many people. And there was an old family friend.

"Pickwick!" she exclaimed.

Waddling up to her, Pickwick confided, "We are the link between the Free Dutch and the British. We also get crews from downed British planes back to England. There's a lot of sympathy here for your work, too." And suddenly he introduced her to the group. "Miss Corrie Smit is the head of an operation rescuing Jews here in Haarlem."

In a daze she whispered, "Me? The head of an operation? And I'm certainly not Corrie Smit."

"We have no other last names in the underground, Corrie Smit," said Pickwick soberly. He smiled. "Peter is going to be released. Cheer up."

How did Pickwick know ahead of time that Peter was going to be released? He must have been powerful indeed, thought Corrie.

It was just a few days later that a frail man with a goatee came to the Beje. Corrie had been told about him at the underground meeting. Of course, he was named Smit.

Papa was unaware of his significance. "Mr. Smit, heh? I knew some Smits in Amsterdam."

Mr. Smit was soon exploring the house. "This structure is a dream come true," he said. "Never have I seen such a hodgepodge of rooms."

"We prefer to think of it as unique," said Corrie, not the least bothered by his remark. She could always take a joke, even one that cut.

The structure of the home was peculiar. The front part was an old house three stories high that ran deep off Barteljorisstraat, yet was only one room wide. Behind it was joined another old house three stories high and one room wide but just one room deep. The floors of the two houses missed each other by several feet, but the mismatch was obscured by stairs in the seam between the two houses.

He laughed. "Sherlock Holmes couldn't figure this house out. Do you remember his story called 'The Adventure of the Norwood Builder'?"

"No, I'll have to read it," said Corrie.

She wasn't happy when he seemed to focus on her small bedroom on the third floor. He said, "This is perfect. It's high. It gives people time to get up here and hide as the Gestapo sweep through the lower part of the house."

"But this is my bedroom. And it's so small."

One week later Corrie's bedroom was even smaller. The man and his helpers had built a fake brick wall. There was now a small room between the fake wall and the real, outer brick wall. The room was two and a half feet wide by about eight feet long. The new brick wall had been painted yet looked a hundred years old. The paint was peeling and water stained. The original molding was put back. In front of the wall was a dilapidated wooden-backed bookcase. Under the lowest shelf was a sliding door.

"Keep a mattress in your secret room, along with water, hardtack, and vitamins," said Mr. Smit and he left.

Corrie felt very cold. Would the Gestapo ever be in her room scratching the walls, sniffing about like great stinking rats? She must have faith in God. The Gestapo would never find the secret room. It was guarded by God's angels. Yes, in her own mind she would now call it the angels' crib!

The Gestapo was not the only ugly arm of the Nazis. With so many of their own men in uniform fighting the British in Africa, fighting the Russians in the east and occupying unfriendly countries all over Europe, the Germans desperately needed workers for their war factories. So in 1942, German soldiers began to raid Dutch homes.

THERE WAS NOW A SMALL ROOM BETWEEN THE FAKE WALL AND THE REAL, OUTER BRICK WALL.

At any moment in any neighborhood, German soldiers might appear in force to scour every house for Dutch men between the ages of sixteen and thirty. Then with rifles and threats they nudged their captives into waiting trucks. The trucks took the men straight to Germany. To the Dutch it seemed a death sentence.

Such a raid occurred when Corrie, Betsie, and Papa were at Nollie's home to celebrate Flip's birthday. Nollie was still out shopping with her two oldest girls Aty and Elske.

Suddenly Nollie's sons, Peter and Bob, raced into the kitchen. "Soldiers are coming! It's a *razzia!*"

They immediately moved the kitchen table aside and yanked a rug away to expose a trapdoor. It was no more than a potato cellar. They opened the trapdoor and dived below.

Those above had barely replaced the rug and table before soldiers burst into the house. "Where are your men?" one demanded.

Nollie's youngest daughter, Cocky, stepped forward. Grandly she replied, "These are my aunts, and this is my grandfather. My father is still at school where he is the principal. My mother is shopping."

The German soldier exploded, "I didn't ask for a family history! Do you have brothers?"

"Yes."

"How old?"

"Twenty-one, nineteen, eighteen."

> COCKY SIGHED. "THEY ARE UNDER THE TABLE."

"Excellent." The soldier actually smiled. "Aren't you the good little girl? Now be a good girl and tell me where they are."

"My oldest brother, Fred, is at theological school."

"And where are the other two?" he asked impatiently.

Corrie held her breath. How long could Cocky have evaded that horrible ultimate question? Corrie felt sick. Nollie couldn't tell a lie, and Cocky was just like her. But surely Cocky wouldn't give up her dear brothers to the Nazis—and to a death sentence in the war factories in Germany!

Cocky sighed. "They are under the table."

The soldier yanked away the tablecloth and peeked under the table, rifle ready. He blinked at empty space. "Don't think we are fools!" he snapped angrily.

Within moments the soldiers were gone, terrorizing the next house. The van Woerdens and ten Booms had more than Flip's birthday to celebrate that afternoon. They celebrated the narrow escape, but during the party Corrie argued with Nollie about telling lies. Nollie insisted a godly person must tell the truth. Corrie didn't agree. She already knew what Peter thought. He had encouraged Corrie to lie about the second radio. How terribly evil the Nazis were to force people into such moral dilemmas. They were demons.

Flip wouldn't take sides. He was thankful, but his face was white as bleached celery with worry. "We were very lucky they were such young soldiers. They never even questioned Katrien."

Corrie knew he was right. Katrien would not fool anyone for very long. She was much older than Annaliese. She looked Semitic. And she knew nothing about actual maid work. She did not even have false papers. The Gestapo would see through Katrien in a flash.

Living with Nazis among them was a never-ending nightmare. Corrie remembered the first motto of her girls' clubs: Seek your strength through prayer. She could find the strength from God. And she needed it. The Beje was as dangerous as Nollie's house. They were hiding Jews at the Beje all the time, too.

Good news crackled over the radio from Britain in January of 1943. The hearts of the Dutch soared. The Russians had stopped the German advance eastward and were even thought to be turning them back! The new year really seemed a turning point in the devil Hitler's fortunes. The British and Americans had routed the Germans from North Africa. At long last the sleeping giant America was fighting. If Hitler expected any help from his Japanese allies, he would not get it. They were being pummeled by the Americans in the Pacific. Glory to God, there was hope for Holland at last.

As if to remind Corrie that a few battles won against the devil did not mean the war was over, that winter in Holland was long and severe. Poor old Christoffels froze to death in his bed in a rooming house, the water in his washbasin frozen solid as rock.

Food and fuel were in short supply all winter. And so were safe havens for Jews while the underground sought farms for them. And even the few havens like the Beje and Mrs. De Boer's attic were not so safe. Mrs. De Boer's house was just four blocks away from the Beje. What happened at her attic was a perfect example of how everything could suddenly go wrong.

9.
THE MORAL DILEMMA

Nineteen Jews were crowded into Mrs. De Boer's attic, but some people simply cannot stay confined indefinitely. Especially if they are young and the smell of spring seeps through the eaves. Eight of the young Jews in a wild impulse took to the streets of Haarlem in the night. Before dawn, all nineteen Jews and Mrs. De Boer herself had disappeared in the deadly clutches of the Gestapo.

Betsie was sad. "It could happen to us. We, too, have a good-sized operation."

Corrie shook her head. "And now we must get bigger."

The operation at Beje expanded. More and more, Corrie became the command center, and more and more Dutch joined Corrie. It seemed that she always needed more messengers and more people with special skills. A fugitive would sicken and die, so Corrie needed a burial. A pregnant Jewish woman's water would break, so Corrie needed a doctor immediately! She needed transportation for fugitives, identification papers for fugitives, food ration books for fugitives. Soon she had eighty people working directly in her operation.

CORRIE SOON HAD EIGHTY PEOPLE WORKING DIRECTLY IN HER OPERATION.

A distribution center for fleeing Jews and Dutch men got special treatment from the Dutch underground. The Beje's phone connection was restored. A buzzer was installed which sounded at the top of the house to warn their fugitives to get to the secret room at once. Buttons which triggered the buzzer were scattered through the lower part of the house, all hidden. But those conveniences came with a heavy price.

"If the phone and alarm system are ever discovered by the Gestapo, they have concrete evidence that we ten Booms are the worst of traitors to the goals of the glorious Third Reich," worried Corrie.

"And the most loyal of the faithful to God's glory," countered Betsie.

More and more people knew about the Beje. More and more Nazi edicts were violated by Corrie and her cohorts. More and more fugitives became difficult to distribute. Some of their Jews simply could not be moved to farms. They looked too Jewish. The farmers would not jeopardize themselves, their families, and their other fugitives to hide such obvious Jews. *Another horrible moral dilemma,* thought Corrie. What wrong was more right in such evil times? Could she blame farmers who were risking so much anyway for the Jews? The rejection wasn't always because of the way a Jew looked; it might be because of something else that made the fugitive too conspicuous: a rattling cough, a pregnancy.

The first of the Beje's new permanent residents was Meyer Mossel. He was their first "watch with a face that needs repair," their underground code for a fugitive too Semitic looking. He not only looked Semitic but was uncompromisingly orthodox with long sideburns. The farmer who was hiding Meyer's son and wife would not take him.

Meyer Mossel looked at Papa in his long white beard. "One of the patriarchs!"

Papa responded, "And I am a brother of the chosen people."

He and Papa were immediate friends. Meyer was a godsend to Papa. He had been a cantor in the synagogue. The Old Testament was heavenly when Meyer read it. And he knew scripture backward and forward, like Papa did. He also had a wonderful sense of humor about himself. In that way he was like Corrie. Jews like Meyer kept Corrie from feeling like a martyr. He was a joy to have in the Beje. It was no great sacrifice to hide such a charming man.

Not all the permanent residents were Jews. Papa's apprentice Jop could no longer travel about in the day. Boys his age were immediately seized and sent to Germany for the war factories. So young Jop became a permanent resident. Also there were Henk, a young lawyer, and Leendert, a teacher. They were hiding at the Beje for the same reason.

Fugitives were coming to the Beje all the time to stay a short time. And they were slipped away in the night to go to some farm. A number could not be placed. So the permanent residents grew to seven. The most dangerous was seventy-six-year-old Mary. Her asthma made her wheeze and cough uncontrollably.

After rising in the morning, all who were in hiding had to drag their bedding, nightclothes, and toilet articles up to the angels' crib. These were exchanged for their day things. Just before bed they exchanged their day things for their night things. This was routine.

They began to drill for the unexpected. It was no game. If only one were caught by the Gestapo they were all caught. So they drilled. The underground had warned Corrie the Gestapo liked to strike at mealtimes and in the middle of the night. The villains especially looked for wastebaskets and ash trays. At night the Gestapo felt every mattress for warmth. They slithered around like snakes.

The Beje drilled for a raid at mealtime. The buzzer sounded unexpectedly. All those in hiding grabbed their dishes and huffed up the stairs. The first time it took them four minutes to disappear into the secret room. A man experienced in the underground acted the part of the Gestapo. He searched the Beje. On the kitchen table were two unexplained spoons, on the stairs was a carrot, and in one of the bedrooms were ashes from Meyer's pipe. The man scowled. It was fatally obvious they were hiding people. They would have to do much better.

So they practiced and practiced until they cut the time to two minutes and left nothing incriminating behind. Then they practiced more. Their goal was one minute. The task was not made any easier by having constant additions to the household. That was why they could never stop practicing. Slowly they brought the time down: ninety seconds, eighty seconds, seventy seconds.

Papa, Toos, and Corrie polished techniques to stall the Gestapo as they swept through the watch shop. They prayed it wouldn't be hard to stumble apologetically in front of some eager Nazi underling or to cause some grim Nazi searcher to hesitate with a well-chosen ambiguous remark about a high official in the Gestapo. Betsie practiced the same techniques on the side door to the alley. They must do everything they could to slow down the Gestapo.

Mealtime drills were just half of the drills. The other drills were for night raids. Corrie hated that drill most of all because they did it after she was asleep. She knew those in hiding jumped up, turned their mattresses over so they were cold to the touch, then hustled their night things upstairs to the angels' crib.

"WHERE ARE YOU HIDING THE JEWS?" THEY WOULD SCREAM IN HER FACE.

The part she despised was her

part. They would shake her awake. "Where are you hiding the Jews?" they would scream in her face.

Corrie was a very heavy sleeper. Time and again she blurted something incriminating. It was a long time before she passed her part. How she dreaded the thought of a real raid in the night!

But life in the Beje was not all stress. At night they gathered in Aunt Jans's rooms. It was like old times. They sang. They studied the Bible. They played the pipe organ, the violin, and the piano. They performed plays. They gave each other language lessons. But after awhile the people of Haarlem only had electricity a short time each night. Candles were too precious to use for fun, so the revelers would retreat into the kitchen where Corrie's bicycle was propped up on a stand. A volunteer would pedal wildly to generate electricity for her headlight. In its beam one of them would read a play or a novel to the others. Such were the ways they clung to their sanity in such mad times.

And where was their deliverance? Where was the invasion of Europe? They had waited half of 1940 and all of 1941 and all of 1942 and half of 1943, hoping the British and Americans would come. Where were they? How long could the secret of the Beje last?

Their fear was not unfounded. One day Corrie looked out the dining room window. Cowering in the alley was a woman, confusion and terror written all over her.

"Katrien, of all people!" Corrie rushed down and pulled her inside.

Katrien was babbling. "Your sister has gone crazy."

"Crazy? Nollie?"

"The Gestapo came to the house. And Nollie told them."

"What? What did she tell them?" Corrie's heart sank. *Oh, Nollie. No.*

"She told them right out that Annaliese is a Jew. I ran out the back door."

It was preposterous. But Corrie knew it was true. If the Gestapo asked Nollie a question, she would tell them the truth. It was daylight, a very dangerous time to be riding a bicycle. But Corrie careened frantically across the town square, over the canal on the Grote Haut bridge, and along the Wagenweg. Within ten minutes she leaned her bicycle on a lamppost on Bos en Hoven Straat and waited.

It was true! Out of Nollie's house came Nollie escorted by a strange man in a suit. Behind them with a second strange man was Annaliese, almost limp.

It was not long before the ten Booms learned Nollie was only a short distance away in the jail on Smedestraat. By all reports she was in high spirits, singing hymns. Poor Annaliese was in the old Jewish theater in Amsterdam, awaiting transport to Germany. Were there really death camps there in Germany? That's what people were saying now. It was monstrous, disgraceful, outrageous, intolerable, shameful, scandalous, intolerable—in short, impossible. Yet for anyone who had suffered under Nazis it did not seem impossible at all.

How could Nollie have betrayed sweet Annaliese?

Corrie could just hear Nollie quote Psalm 141:

> *Set a watch, O LORD, before my mouth; keep the door of my lips. Incline not my heart to any evil thing, to practise wicked works with men that work iniquity: and let me not eat of their dainties.*

Nollie could be so righteous! How could Corrie ever forgive her for how she doomed poor Annaliese?

But six days later Pickwick phoned Corrie and in code urged her to rush to his house in the suburb of Aerdenhout. There he told her, "We freed forty Jews from the old Jewish theater in Amsterdam last night. One of them was very anxious that Nollie know about it."

Annaliese was free! So the only harm done was to Nollie. Corrie felt terrible now for berating Nollie. And the news got worse. Nollie was transferred to federal prison in Amsterdam. Poor, sweet Nollie. But Corrie knew no prison could defeat Nollie's spirit. She was much too near God. Oh, how Nollie would frustrate her captors. How her sweet soprano would fill their cold-barred world with hymns.

But Corrie wasn't going to sit on her hands.

> CORRIE KNEW NO PRISON COULD DEFEAT NOLLIE'S SPIRIT. SHE WAS MUCH TOO NEAR GOD.

Following Pickwick's advice, she visited the doctor in charge of the prison hospital. The Beje residents had been reading Dale Carnegie's *How to Win Friends and Influence People.* There were few times in Corrie's life when she wanted to influence anyone more than she did now. And when she saw Doberman pinschers in the waiting room she knew which strategy from Dale Carnegie's book she would use.

"How smart of you, doctor!" she said brightly in German. "You brought those lovely dogs with you to keep you company here in Holland."

"Do you like dogs?" He was suspicious, but what dog lover can resist talking about his incomparable dogs?

Corrie was almost breathless as she rattled on about dogs and sought the doctor's good advice on dogs. Corrie became spellbound by the many excellent qualities of the Dobermans. But the doctor finally tired of bragging and asked, "Why are you here?"

"My sister, Nollie van Woerden, is here." Corrie suddenly decided to be as recklessly honest as Nollie. "She's here for hiding a Jew. My sister has six children."

The doctor stood up. "You must go now."

Corrie went back to the Beje. Had she succeeded in anything at all? She busied herself again in her other dangerous activities, but she was never too busy to stop and wonder, *Will Nollie be released? Is this the day?*

She told herself to be patient. If the doctor was an ally to their cause she must not jeopardize such a valuable man by hanging around asking favors. What if the Beje operation were discovered by the Gestapo? Wouldn't they backtrack Corrie looking for others? Of course they would.

But finally her patience ran out. She returned to the doctor. He grimaced, but then he quickly enthused about dogs again, mentioning a breed that is particularly stubborn. Still smiling, talking about how that breed is not popular these days, he ushered her to the door and said softly, "For heaven's sake, don't come back here again. I must have time for my work."

One night during supper at the Beje, the doorbell to the front door of the shop rang. "It's after curfew!" gasped Meyer. "No one I would want to meet would be on Barteljorisstraat!"

Corrie hurried to the front door. "Otto!" gasped Corrie, with real surprise.

"Yes, it's me." Otto was the German apprentice whom Papa had to fire for his viciousness to Christoffels. He was now a soldier in the German army. His sneering face betrayed he was back to gloat.

Corrie screamed, "I can't believe it. It really is you, Otto!"

"You needn't yell like that." He barged in and began to strut to the back of the shop. "Let's go up to the dining room and discuss old times with the pious old Bible babbler."

"Just one moment. I need to lock the door." Corrie hit the alarm button.

"What was that?" snapped Otto. "It sounded like a buzzer."

"One of the clocks. A buzzer went off accidentally."

Otto rushed to the back of the shop and into the workroom. Corrie hurried behind him. When she came into the kitchen right behind Otto her heart started beating again. All the fugitives were gone. Only Papa and Betsie were at the table. The table was set for only three. The residents of the Beje had dodged a bullet again. But how many bullets could they dodge? Even now Otto was suspicious. Corrie was not acting herself.

Papa humored Otto as he gloated about the successes of the Third Reich. Papa probably actually pitied Otto. And maybe Otto deserved a crumb of pity. It seemed to Corrie that the Germans must be woefully ignorant of their armies being chased out of North Africa and their setbacks in Russia. But where was the invasion from the British and Americans to rescue Europe?

Finally Otto tired of his juvenile game and left.

The ten Booms got an early Christmas present. Nollie was released from prison. Apparently the prison doctor thought her blood pressure was dangerously low. Nollie shrugged. She never doubted God would take care of her.

In December the Beje started to celebrate not Christmas but

PAPA HUMORED OTTO AS HE GLOATED ABOUT THE SUCCESSES OF THE THIRD REICH.

Hanukkah. Betsie found a Hanukkah candlestand and each night they performed the rituals. With Meyer's help their celebration was very authentic. And joyous. And loud. Corrie was chilled when the wife of the optician who lived next door asked discreetly if they could sing with a little less volume. So their neighbors knew! Who else knew? Who walking by in the street might hear their Jewish festivities? How close was the Beje to discovery?

In January of 1944, Corrie was jolted. She received a message to come to the police station on Smedestraat. She was baffled. That was not the way the Gestapo operated. But what was she to think? Nollie's captivity had not gone to waste. Corrie first packed a prison bag. In it went a Bible, a pencil, needle and thread, soap, toothbrush, and comb. She took a leisurely bath then dressed in several sets of underwear and her warmest clothing topped by two sweaters. Then she trudged—no innocent—to the police station.

The chief of police himself wanted to talk to her. After she entered his office he closed the door. The two were alone. He was a brusque man. He didn't waste any time. He turned the volume up on a radio and leaned forward, barely talking loud enough for her to hear him only inches away.

"I know all about you and your other work," he mouthed.

"My work with disabled children?" she asked evasively.

"No," he said. "Never mind. I'm not trying to force you to admit it, but I do know you're working in the underground with the Free Dutch. I have someone I need silenced—permanently. Can you give me the name of someone in the underground who can take care of my problem?"

The chief was Dutch, a native of Haarlem. But had he been corrupted by the Gestapo? What should she do? Why would such a man, who knew the name of every roach in Haarlem that crawled under a rock, need her help? Surely it was a trap.

She said, "My role is to free lips not silence them. I can't help you. But I will pray with you that this problem is removed from your life. And I will pray that no one has to be silenced."

The chief prayed with her. He was much too taciturn for her to know if he was trying to trick her or not. She returned to the Beje, not confident at all. The activity at the Beje was becoming too obvious. If the chief really had a spy in his office, how long would the Beje's secret last? And so many people now just came to her off the street, always asking for help. Could she hide a Jewish woman and her baby? Could she find a place for a Dutch boy to hide? Could she give them guilders to bribe a policeman? Could she get a message to someone in jail? And who was to know if the plea was coming from a spy for the Gestapo? And could she ever refuse to help someone?

Just weeks later the apprentice Jop was captured. He was bicycling on an errand for Corrie. It had to happen sooner or later. But unfortunately Jop was not caught en route. He was caught at an underground house. How could a seventeen-year-old like Jop hold up to torture by the Gestapo?

HOW MUCH LONGER COULD THE AMATEURS IN THE DUTCH UNDERGROUND HOLD OUT AGAINST RUTHLESS SNAKES OF THE THIRD REICH?

Each day now seemed more treacherous than the last. And to compound the agony, Corrie came down with the flu. She lay under her vaporizer, aching with every breath. Oh, how she longed to hear the radio exultantly announce the British and Americans were storming the shores of France! It was February of 1944. The Nazis had infested Holland for almost four years! How much longer could the amateurs in the Dutch underground hold out against ruthless snakes of the Third Reich? How horrible Corrie felt.

What was that sound? Thumping feet? Was she dreaming or was this real? Were those frantic whispers she heard? Had she heard the buzzer? She struggled to rise.

"Is this finally the end?" she mumbled groggily.

10.
CAUGHT!

Bodies were scrambling under her bookcase!

"Yes!" blurted Corrie. "This nightmare is real!"

How many had entered the angels' crib? Then Mary appeared, slumped in the doorway, gasping for air. She had to be the last one.

Corrie jumped from the bed, her head booming pain with every heart beat. She rudely shoved Mary under the bookcase. A man she had never seen before scrambled in after Mary. So Mary wasn't the last one. Corrie slammed the sliding door shut. She arose on wobbly legs and toppled back into bed.

Voices came from below: harsh, demanding. In German. *"Schnell!"* Thumps. *"Passen sie auf!"* Nasty even for a German soldier. *"Wo sind die Juden?"* No, these weren't soldiers. The Gestapo!

In between the shrill barks below came a sound from the secret room: wheezing! It was Mary. Was she really that loud? Yes. It was definitely Mary, breathing like a freight train.

"Oh please, Jesus, heal Mary. Now! I know You can do it," cried Corrie.

NASTY EVEN FOR A GERMAN SOLDIER.

"Was is das!" A man rushed into the bedroom. "Who are you talking to?" he barked in Dutch.

"No one you would know," mumbled Corrie as she clutched the covers around her.

"What did you say?" he growled.

"Why are you here?" asked Corrie, clutching the covers tighter.

"I ask the questions here!" The man wore a blue suit. He was tall but portly, with a pasty face. "What is your name?"

"Cornelia ten Boom."

"Prove it."

She opened the pouch she wore around her neck. She pulled out her identification folder. "Here."

He yanked it from her hand and checked a notebook. "So it is you!" He threw the folder back in her face.

"Why are you here?" She coughed at him with all her might.

"Cover your mouth! Have some decency." He backed up. "What is that smell? Menthol? Camphor? Get up at once and get out of here." He backed up through the door. "Your room smells like a sewer. You really are sick, aren't you?" His pasty face sagged with revulsion. "Come downstairs at once. And no funny business." He held a handkerchief over his nose and mouth. "This is such a dirty business at times," he complained to himself.

Corrie lurched to her feet. "Let me dress, please."

"Hurry up!"

She wanted to get out of the room as fast as possible herself. Mary might start wheezing any moment. She tugged clothes over her pajamas. She struggled to put on two sweaters.

"I said no funny business!" he barked.

"I have the chills," she said. She grabbed her winter coat. Where was her precious prison bag?

Her prison bag was by the sliding door!

How could she have been so careless? She couldn't draw attention to it now. What if Mary coughed or wheezed just then?

Corrie had to keep coughing herself. The man might not notice an extra cough or wheeze. But how could she draw attention to the door? Yet how could she leave her precious bag? Prison would be hell without it. But she couldn't take the chance. She had to get out of her bedroom as soon as possible. The man was repelled by her room, yet now he seemed torn. He inched closer, as if he should really stay and poke around for a while. And what if Mary coughed? Corrie lurched out of the room and stumbled down the stairs.

"Be careful," said the man. "Cover your mouth."

A soldier stood in front of Aunt Jans's rooms. Hadn't there been a prayer meeting there earlier? It was Willem's meeting. It was for real. It gave Willem an excuse to keep coming to Haarlem. Even Nollie and Peter were in his prayer meetings. Oh, surely they were gone by now. What time was it? How long had she slept? What day was it?

In the dining room, a man in a brown suit sat at the table. Corrie cried, "Papa. Betsie. Toos." They were sitting on chairs against the wall. Beside them were three workers from the underground. Corrie could see daylight out the dining room window.

The pasty-faced man in the blue suit said in German, "I've got Cornelia ten Boom here." He paused for effect. "The ringleader," he sneered.

"Ringleader?" answered the man at the table in German. He looked up. He had been counting silver coins hidden under the staircase with the radio. "That old frump?" He shrugged. "Take her downstairs and find out where the Jews are hidden." He shivered and glanced toward the barren coal hearth. It rarely had a fire these days. "You people live like barbarians. I'm surprised you have chairs." He began counting again.

The man in the blue suit prodded Corrie through the workroom into the front showroom. He slapped her hard. "Attention now!"

She held her stinging face. "What do you want?"

"Where are you hiding the Jews?"

"We have none."

He slapped her again. "Where are the stolen ration books?"

"We don't have any—"

He slapped her again. "Where are you hiding the Jews?"

> HE SLAPPED HER AGAIN. "WHERE ARE YOU HIDING THE JEWS?"

"Oh, please, Jesus, stop him." She was coughing. She tasted blood in her mouth.

He lowered his arm and backed up. "What do you have? It's not tuberculosis, is it? What a dirty business this is." He scowled at his notebook again. "Which one is Elizabeth?"

Soon Corrie sat in Betsie's chair in the dining room and Betsie was in the showroom taking the blows from the man in the blue suit.

But soon she was back, slender and limp, lips trembling and swollen. Corrie rose and helped sit her down. Betsie whispered, "I feel sorry for that man."

A woman blundered in the alley door. "They arrested Herman Sluring!"

"Quiet!" screamed Corrie.

"You be quiet!" The man in the blue suit struck Corrie.

The man at the table glared at her. "We might have learned something from that silly fool," he said to the other man in German. "Bring her up here."

But the woman froze. Now she knew she was in the hands of the Gestapo. Corrie was depressed. So they had arrested Pickwick, too. And there was Papa. *Please, Lord Jesus, don't let them hurt Papa.* She heard noises of splintering wood above them. Had they found the room? But there were no screams. No cries of triumph. Perhaps not.

So far the Gestapo had found the hidden silver, which was supposed to have been surrendered to the Nazis long ago. They found the radio, the telephone, even the alarm system. Only a fool would have not realized the ten Booms were in very deep trouble. There would be no evading Nazi injustice for these violations.

A man blundered in the alley door. He was arrested. Then another man. Finally the traffic stopped. The word was out. The Beje had been raided.

The man at the table stood up. "I guess we can leave now," he said in Dutch. He smiled evilly at Corrie. "Aren't you happy? Your Jewish roaches are safe, aren't they? Well, when you are rotting in prison, reflect on this. We will surround your house for as long as it takes. The Jewish roaches in your secret room will turn into mummies. It will be a very long, very painful death!"

But Corrie was happy. The Gestapo had not found the secret room. There was still hope for the people in the angels' crib. The Gestapo had failed!

Suddenly captives began filing out of Aunt Jans's room, past the dining room and down the stairs. There was Nollie! And Peter! and Willem! Every ten Boom. Thank God Mama had not lived to see this awful day.

And yet all the way down the alley and the half block up Smedestraat to the

THE GESTAPO HAD NOT FOUND THE SECRET ROOM. THERE WAS STILL HOPE FOR THE PEOPLE IN THE ANGELS' CRIB.

police station Corrie thanked Jesus for helping them. Mary had not made any noise in all that time. Their fugitives were still safe.

Inside the station, not police but soldiers herded them down a corridor into a gymnasium. Thirty-five people had been arrested at the Beje. The men of the Gestapo looked very proud. This was quite a roundup for them—so large, they would probably brag, that they needed a gymnasium to hold all the criminals. Would the two men in suits be thinking of promotions? What normal person could know what went through such sick Nazi minds?

In the gymnasium, the captives could talk among themselves. They even used the toilets off the gymnasium to flush papers that should not be discovered. So the Gestapo was not so smart after all. Just active and evil.

That night ended just as almost every night of Corrie's life ended. In a deep steady voice Papa delivered the word of God:

SO THE GESTAPO WAS NOT SO SMART AFTER ALL. JUST ACTIVE AND EVIL.

He that dwelleth in the secret place of the most High shall abide under the shadow of the Almighty. I will say of the LORD, He is my refuge and my fortress: my God; in him will I trust. Surely he shall deliver thee from the snare of the fowler, and from the noisome pestilence. He shall cover thee with his feathers, and under his wings shalt thou trust: his truth shall be thy shield and buckler. Thou shalt not be afraid for the terror by night; nor for the arrow that flieth by day; nor for the pestilence that walketh in darkness; nor for the destruction that wasteth at noonday. A thousand shall fall at thy side, and ten thousand at thy right

*hand; but it shall not come nigh thee. Only with thine
eyes shalt thou behold and see the reward of the wicked.
Because thou hast made the L*ORD*, which is my refuge,
even the most High, thy habitation; there shall no
evil befall thee, neither shall any plague come nigh thy
dwelling. For he shall give his angels charge over thee,
to keep thee in all thy ways. They shall bear thee up in
their hands, lest thou dash thy foot against a stone. Thou
shalt tread upon the lion and adder: the young lion and
the dragon shalt thou trample under feet. Because he
hath set his love upon me, therefore will I deliver him: I
will set him on high, because he hath known my name.
He shall call upon me, and I will answer him: I will
be with him in trouble; I will deliver him, and honour
him. With long life will I satisfy him, and shew him
my salvation.*

Psalm 91 had never seemed more appropriate. It was wonderful to be in the company of David.

The next morning they were marched out of the police station. In the street waited a long green bus. Some soldiers were already inside it. Suddenly Herman Sluring was swept past Corrie. She hadn't even known Pickwick was in the police station. He was hatless. His bald head and face were mottled with angry red welts. Corrie squeezed onto one double seat with Papa and Betsie. As the driver ground the gears and the bus labored away, Corrie saw Willem's wife, Tine, in the crowd of stunned gaucheries along the sidewalk.

The green bus rumbled across the town square. In the bus were Corrie, Papa, Betsie. The bus was crowded. Farther back were Nollie, Willem, and Peter, Pickwick, and Toos. Each one of them wanted to get off but couldn't. Corrie remembered her vision the night of the Nazi invasion. They were being taken away against their will in a wagon drawn by enormous black horses. Now she knew what it meant. Her vision of May 10, 1940, had come true February 29, 1944.

"February 29," whispered Corrie to Betsie, "is good. It's one anniversary I don't want to have every year."

It was a bright winter day. The bus headed not east to Amsterdam but south along the dunes that held back the North Sea. In two hours, the bus was rumbling through the streets of The Hague.

In Dutch, Willem said, "The Hague has the headquarters of the Gestapo for all of Holland."

Inside the headquarters was not terror but grinding bureaucracy. The men in suits were now clerks for the Gestapo, behind a high counter, asking questions and typing answers onto papers. One answer was never enough. Every question had to be asked a dozen times—not as a shrewd tool of interrogation but the result of an over-reaching fumbling bureaucracy. Was this the true hell behind the Nazis? Were they a collection of cold-blooded petty clerks? It was almost funny. If Corrie had not been so sick with the flu she probably would have laughed. How could anyone respect such fools?

There was a fuss when Papa reached the front of the line. "Was it necessary to arrest this old man?" boomed an official who seemed to be the head of the bureaucratic madness.

"He is one of the ringleaders," blinked the man in the brown suit.

"We don't want old codgers like him in our system," growled the head man in German. "Let someone else take care of him." He leaned over to

> "IF I GO HOME," SAID PAPA, "I WILL OPEN MY DOOR AGAIN TO ANYONE WHO KNOCKS."

Papa. He shouted in Dutch, "Listen up, old man. If I send you home will you behave yourself?"

"If I go home," said Papa, "I will open my door again to anyone who knocks."

The head man's face reddened. In German he barked, "Type this fool's papers!"

"It is an honor to go to prison for God's people," persisted Papa. "I pity you."

Many hours later soldiers prodded them into the back of a canvas-topped army truck. They bounced and rattled on a long ride. But more than soon enough, massive gates clanged behind them. Where were they? Corrie could see nothing.

In a loud voice, Willem said, "We are at the federal prison in Scheveningen."

They scrambled down out of the truck to stand dazed in a courtyard surrounded by high, brick walls. Soldiers prodded them inside a long, low building. They lined up facing a wall inches from their noses.

"Women prisoners, follow me!" screamed a woman's voice.

Corrie turned, blinking into the bright ceiling lights. There was Papa not far away, sitting very erect in a high-backed chair.

"Good-bye, Papa. God be with you," cried Corrie.

"God be with you, Papa," echoed Betsie.

"And God goes with you, my daughters," Papa said in a voice that was clear but thin with exhaustion.

Corrie looked desperately for Willem and Peter. Where were they? A soldier approached with a rifle. She must keep moving. She held Betsie's hand and rushed ahead with the flow of prisoners. Where was Nollie? Then she saw Nollie just ahead.

A door banged behind them. Coconut-palm matting ran down the center of the hallway. It sponged under her tired legs.

The prisoners were urged along by women guards, armed with billy clubs.

"Follow the matron—but keep off the mat!" barked a guard. "Prisoners never walk on the mats."

The flow stopped. They waited their turn to once again give their names to a woman at a desk in the hallway. But this time they were ordered to surrender anything of value. Corrie gave up her Alpina wristwatch, a gold ring, and a few Dutch guilders. Her belongings disappeared into a large envelope.

Now they marched down the cold hallway scarred by narrow metal doors, stopping only for the matron to unlock a door and a guard to roughly shove one of the women inside. Betsie was the first sister to go into a cell. Nollie went in a cell two doors beyond Betsie's cell. If only Corrie were next. She would at least be close to her dear sisters.

FOUR WOMEN WERE IMPRISONED IN THE CELL WITH ONE COT. THREE THIN MATS WERE ON THE FLOOR.

But they went on and on, turned a corner, turned another corner, and then another, until Corrie was hopelessly disoriented. Finally a guard shoved her stumbling inside a cell. Four women were imprisoned in the cell with one cot. Three thin mats were on the floor.

The matron snapped, "Give this prisoner the cot."

Corrie began coughing.

"Don't put a sick woman in with us," whined one of the inmates.

But they were not all so rude and selfish. Corrie was even comforted by one of the cellmates after she collapsed on the cot, clutching her coat around her aching body against the clammy air.

Later a hand struck her. "Wake up. It's food call," said a voice.

Corrie sat up. A square of metal dropped down in the door, forming a shelf. Four tin plates heaped with steaming gruel were placed there on the shelf.

"We get an extra portion," screamed one of the inmates. "We have a new one in here!"

Corrie looked away from the watery porridge. "I can't eat now." And she collapsed again. The grumbling subsided as the four divided up her portion. When they finished, they put their plates back on the food shelf.

It didn't take long to learn prison routine. Once a day they got hot food, usually gruel. Once a day they got a piece of dark bread. Once a day they passed out the bucket they had to use for a toilet. It was returned empty. Once a day they passed out the wash basin full of gray water. It was returned with clean water.

All day long, one of the women walked the length of the narrow cell. Six steps from end to end. One naked light bulb burned overhead. There were no windows.

In spite of her illness, Corrie tried to talk to the women. They were curt. They guarded their pasts. Their universe now was prison. It was only painful to speak of the outside. Would Corrie get that way?

A noise rattled in the hall. Feet padded in the hall, too. "That's a trusty with the medical cart. Someone is sick," said one woman.

A door opened. There were footsteps.

"That's the matron," said the same woman. "I'll bet she found someone with an extra blanket."

A door opened and closed somewhere in the hall. There were footsteps.

"That's someone in 316 being led away by a guard. Toward the interior. For a hearing," said the same woman.

"How can you know all that?" asked Corrie, unbelieving.

"We get four kind of visitors," said the same woman in a resigned voice. "Trusties are not too bad. Guards are usually bad. The matron almost always brings bad news. And a soldier puts your heart in your mouth."

"But how can you know so much?" asked Corrie.

"She's been here three years," snarled one of the other cellmates bitterly.

One of these women had been here three years! Corrie found that fact so depressing she shut up. A hunted animal didn't have senses finer tuned than the woman who had been here three years. She knew every sound. How the woman must have longed for freedom. Or had she given up? It seemed useless to ask.

Corrie thought about Papa. What a miserable place this was. How would her dear Papa survive this? He was eighty-four. She always felt he lived on because he was buoyed up by love and friendship in the Beje. How would he do now?

> WHAT A MISERABLE PLACE THIS WAS. HOW WOULD HER DEAR PAPA SURVIVE THIS?

The boredom became a challenge. One of the women played solitaire all day. The ten Booms had never played cards. But Corrie gave it a try. Solitaire was fun. But she began to use the game like a ouija board. If the cards were good, that meant good news was coming. If the cards were bad, that meant nothing at all was going to happen. After a while the card game seemed so devilish she had to stop playing.

She wasn't getting her health back. As often as not she was limp as a rag on the cot, coughing and aching.

One day in her second week of imprisonment the matron unlocked the door. "Get your hat and coat, ten Boom!"

"Something unusual is up!" blurted the inmate who had been there three years. Her mouth was gaping.

"Good or bad?" asked Corrie.

"Shut up, prisoner!" growled the matron. "Come with me."

What was it? Was something waiting for Corrie too horrible to imagine?

11.
IMPRISONED

Corrie would not allow herself to think the worst. "Are you freeing me?" she asked.

"Shut up, prisoner!"

Oh God, if freedom is Your will, please let it be true. How Corrie hated the cell. And using the bucket in front of the others was so degrading. It was awful. Why couldn't she be free? Nollie had been freed from a federal prison after admitting she hid a Jew. Of course it was true. Oh, it was wonderful to be out of the cell. She refused to think about the worst possibility.

"Stay off the mat!" barked the matron.

Corrie almost felt good as she stepped out into the courtyard with the high brick walls. She gazed at the marvelous blue sky.

"Get your nose out of the clouds!" snapped the matron. "Get in the automobile."

The matron shoved Corrie in the back seat of a black automobile next to a soldier and woman who looked sick. In the front seat was the driver and a man who was also sick, his head lolling back like his neck was a rag. The massive gates swung open and the automobile sped through.

They drove into The Hague. Dutch people were actually strolling the sidewalks. How precious. Were they thankful? Corrie would like to find out for herself. She tried not to think about the headquarters of the Gestapo.

Soon they stopped at a building. The sign said it was a medical clinic. They were escorted into a room full of waiting people. So that was it. They were being taken to a doctor. The soldier watched them. When Corrie asked him for permission to use the bathroom he had a nurse take her.

Inside the bathroom, the nurse whispered, "Can I get you anything?"

"Did you treat Casper ten Boom? Can you find out what happened to him?"

"I meant *things!*" the nurse whispered in exasperation.

"I need most of all a Bible. And also a. . .a needle and thread. And soap. And a toothbrush."

"I must go. Hurry up or the soldier will be hammering in the door."

> "I NEED MOST OF ALL A BIBLE. AND SOAP. AND A TOOTHBRUSH."

Was it possible the nurse would actually get Corrie those things? Was it a trap? No. It was too brusque. Too rushed. Why should she doubt it? There were Dutch people everywhere trying to block the Nazis in small but dangerous ways.

After the doctor had taken her temperature and listened to her chest with his stethoscope, he diagnosed pleurisy. The nurse returned her to the soldier, pressing something into her hand. It was wrapped in paper. Corrie shoved it into her coat pocket. Did she have all she asked for? It seemed miraculous. But the miracle faded as she realized she was being returned to prison.

"It is you. You're back!" exclaimed the woman whose hearing had been acutely tuned for three years. "Where did you go?"

"A medical clinic." Corrie waited to hear the door lock and

footsteps retreat down the hallway. Then she pulled out the bundle. "I have something." She unwrapped it. "Soap!" She held up two bars. "Who wants to wash first?" The soap was snatched out of her hand. She held up a packet. "Look, safety pins."

"What treasure," said one of the inmates.

"Finally, the best of all," said Corrie. "The gospels." She held up four tiny books.

The others drew back. "Are you crazy? If you get caught—"

"What? *Kalte kost* for that, too?" asked Corrie in a tired voice. It seemed every infraction in prison was punished by *kalte kost*, which meant only cold food was given to the prisoner. And that meant only bread, no hot gruel, as bad as that was.

The one who had been there three years shook her head. "If you're caught with a Bible, the Nazis double your sentence!"

That punishment took Corrie's breath away. "How the Nazis fear the Bible!"

And just two days later the matron entered again. "Get your hat and coat, ten Boom!"

"Something's up again," said the astonished inmate who had been there three years.

"Stay off the mat!" snapped the matron in the hallway.

Had a cellmate squealed on Corrie? Surely there was no reason to call her out of the cell again. And sure enough she was not heading for the courtyard and freedom. She was walking deeper into the prison. The matron finally stopped and unlocked the door of a cell.

"Get inside."

Corrie entered an empty cell. The door slammed behind her. The cot smelled foul. Yes, someone had vomited on it. She felt very sick. The stench seemed to trigger something because she became very sick, even feverish. She was so sick she collapsed on the stinking cot and couldn't even get up to get her food when later it came through the slot in the door.

She cried to the retreating footsteps, "Did the doctor tell you I am dying?"

Was that why she had been moved? So she could die alone in a filthy cell? Was this to be her final scene on earth? The second time they brought food a hand hurled a hunk of bread toward the cot. Next morning a woman actually entered the cell to bring hot food to her cot.

A medical trusty visited her. He gave her a dose of medicine that tasted as foul as it looked then took her temperature. All of the menial work was done by trusties. She asked the trusty about Papa, but the trusty would not talk to her. She already knew he wouldn't from her former cellmates. After all, they were trusties. They were not about to jeopardize their privileged positions, whatever that got them. Corrie was sure she would never be a trusty.

WAS THAT WHY SHE HAD BEEN MOVED? SO SHE COULD DIE ALONE IN A FILTHY CELL?

For a while the medical trusty came every day. Finally he stopped coming. And the woman no longer brought hot food to her. In fact, whoever brought the food now abused her. "I know you have no fever. Get off the bed. Do you think you are a privileged princess?"

Corrie did begin to feel better. She knew now she was in an outside cell. It was much colder than the other cell. And why not? There was a barred window high above her, open to the outside. Oh, what if Papa had been locked in such a cell? March had been bitterly cold. It was now April. She had been in prison one month.

She had never reflected much on weather. It was hard to imagine a country that had weather easier to predict than Holland's.

It varied so little. From midnight to afternoon the temperature ranged a mere ten degrees. Along the coast in places like Haarlem and here at Scheveningen many days were sunny. In the hottest part of summer, temperature hit a maximum of about seventy during the day and dropped to sixty at night. In the coldest blast of winter the temperature dropped just to freezing at night and rose to about forty during the day. Corrie had been lucky. During the very coldest weather she had been in an interior cell. If she had been in this cell the first week, she probably would have died.

"Praise God," she said to the blue sky through the barred window, "for fair weather."

> WHAT HAD HAPPENED TO ALL HER COHORTS? WHAT ABOUT THE FUGITIVES IN THE ANGELS' CRIB?

As the weather improved, the window became an ally. For one hour a day, a ray of sunshine swept the lower reaches of the cell. Corrie bathed in it. It made her feel healthy again. But health brought memories back. Worry over Papa crushed her. And the collapse of her Beje underground was a terrible worry. What had happened to all her cohorts? And what about the fugitives in the angels' crib?

She had neglected her precious gospels. But she had no choice. Her eyes had been so bad. Praise God, Papa had encouraged her to memorize verses. That satisfied her hunger for the Bible. Now she was well enough to read again. She read constantly. The gospels rejuvenated her more than the sunshine. How could she have sunk so low? What seemed like failure could be a colossal success. Her spirits rose.

Her birthday came and passed, observed by no one. But she did get a treat two days later on April 17: her first shower in six weeks.

Other prisoners were showering, too. What a joy it was to see and hear other women. She had been in solitary for one month. She resolved to bring three of her gospels with her when she took her next shower and give them away. How could she hoard such a treasure for herself?

She was feeling much better. How had she survived? Praise God.

Life seemed to spring from God's grace now. An ant scurried out of a crack in the floor. It was a major event. Corrie felt honored. It had seemed for a while no life was low enough to visit such a cell as hers. But now she had an ant visiting, a forerunner of better things. She scattered bread crumbs on the floor by the crack. She must make sure the ant returned. And it did. She now had three wonderful gifts: the sunshine, the ant, and the gospels.

Then she received a package! Nothing was written on it but Corrie's name and the address of the prison, but Corrie knew it was from Nollie's family, the van Woerdens. In it were sandwiches, a brown cake, and a pan of porridge. And there was much more: a needle and thread, two bottles of vitamins, and a brilliant red towel! How Nollie's family understood prisons now.

"Inmates in this gray hell crave color," she told the ant.

She wrote a letter thanking the van Woerdens for the package, assuring them she was recovering from pleurisy, and putting her solitary confinement in a positive light: gregarious nonstop Corrie was forced to stop and see deep inside herself, to see her sin. Praise God. She knew now she was entitled to write one letter every three weeks. When had she found out? She couldn't even remember. And she wasn't sure she could have written earlier anyway. Her eyes were too poor. And her spirits had been poor, too. She had not appreciated God's plan for her then. It was good she hadn't written.

The evening of April 20 was very unusual. For seven weeks the prison had been like a tomb. Usually she had to strain to hear anything more than padding feet and squeaking cart wheels. But this evening she heard shouts. Yes, actual shouts. What was it? She was very lucky. The food shelf in her door had been left open. She pressed her ear against the opening.

"What is it?" shouted someone. "Where are the guards? Are we being rescued? Are the British and Americans here at last?"

"You might as well hope for a visit from the queen," answered a voice choked with bitterness. "It's Hitler's birthday. The guards are celebrating with the other miserable Nazis."

"Don't waste this time complaining," urged another voice. "We can exchange information."

What happened next was miraculous to Corrie. Somehow these poor, lost souls organized and disciplined themselves to spread news all around the prison.

"I'M CORRIE TEN BOOM IN CELL 384. WHERE ARE THE TEN BOOMS: BETSIE AND CASPER AND WILLEM?"

"I'm Corrie ten Boom in cell 384," yelled Corrie. "Where are the ten Booms: Betsie and Casper and Willem? Where are the van Woerdens: Nollie and Peter?"

And so the messages flew back and forth. It was a glorious time. Especially when news cycled back: Nollie was released! Oh, Nollie. Wouldn't you know it? Nollie always landed on her feet like a cat! Young Peter was released. Praise God for that. Willem was released. Praise the Lord. Herman Sluring was released. Even Pickwick! And Toos! The news stunned Corrie. Had they all been released? Please God, let it be true. Then she heard Betsie was still in cell 312.

That evening soothed much of the ache in her heart. But there still was no news of Papa. One week later another package was thrown into her cell. It was addressed by Nollie! Corrie could tell her handwriting. Inside was Nollie's favorite sweater: pale blue with flowers embroidered over the pocket. How wonderful. And more vitamins. And cookies. Rewrapping her treasures, Corrie noticed something odd about Nollie's handwriting. It seemed slanted toward the stamp. Quickly she worked the stamp loose with water. Yes! There was a message under the stamp!

Corrie whispered the words to herself, "All the watches in your closet are safe."

So the fugitives in the angels' crib in the Beje had escaped! Praise God. Corrie should not have worried about them after being processed by the Gestapo in The Hague. Such bunglers could not sustain a watch around the Beje week after week. Constant vigil was nothing but an empty threat by the Gestapo, hoping she would panic and talk.

She had only one worry now: Papa. Where was he?

One day Corrie was pulling thread from the red towel to embroider colorful figures on her pajamas. Her food shelf opened and something drifted in like a beautiful snowflake. Her very first letter. It was from Nollie! It read:

> *My dear Corrie,*
> *How happy we were with your letter and that the*
> *Lord has heard our prayers and you are at peace and*
> *happy. When I heard you were alone, I was so upset.*
> *Darling, now I have to tell you something very sad.*
> *Be strong.*

No! Not that. Corrie wasn't strong enough for that. Must she read more? How she dreaded to read the next lines. But she must. *Trust God,* she reminded herself. She could wait one month, dying every second, and the letter would still have to be read:

> *On the tenth of March, our dear Papa went to heaven. He survived only nine days. He passed away in Loosduinen. Yesterday I fetched his belongings from Scheveningen. I know the Lord will help you bear this. It was pneumonia. Betsie knows it already and wrote us about it. She already had premonitions about this, years ago.*

So Betsie knew about Papa. Betsie had a real gift, almost a gift for prophecy. And why not? Did Corrie know anyone more in Christ than Betsie? How she wanted to talk to Betsie now. Poor Papa. No, Corrie mustn't grieve in the wrong way. Not with pity or sorrow. She must be sorry only because she missed his wonderful presence. Papa said he would gladly die for the Jews. And he did.

PAPA SAID HE WOULD GLADLY DIE FOR THE JEWS. AND HE DID.

Corrie gathered her thoughts for a letter. She mustn't waste precious opportunities to write.

> *Dear Nollie and all the other loved ones,*
> *On May 3rd I received your letter. First I was sad, but now I am comforted completely. Father can now sing:*
>
> *I cannot do without You,*
> *You Jesus, my Lord,*

Thanks, praise, adoration,
Never will I be without You again.

How beautiful his voice will sound. I am so happy
for him. When I think of those nine days I quickly
switch to the present and concentrate on how happy
he is now for he sees the answer to everything.

As she signed the letter, she realized Papa was now with Mama, too. And dear Aunt Anna. And feisty Aunt Jans. And Aunt Bep. And Papa's father, Willem. And his grandfather Gerrit. What glory. How she wanted to see them, too! Was dying so bad? Hardly. But she remembered Paul's letter to Philippi. No matter how tempting it was to end our trials on earth, it was pure selfishness. One had to fight the good fight for the faith on earth first.

The days dragged on. Corrie thought of many things. But she tried not to think how, of all thirty-five people arrested in February, only she and Betsie were still in prison. But she did think about it. Why was it? Was it because she and Betsie were such notorious members of the Dutch underground? She had to laugh. She didn't have one-tenth the influence that Pickwick had. So why were she and Betsie still in prison? Poor, sweet Betsie. She had only helped like the others. She wasn't in the center of the storm like Corrie. Maybe Corrie did belong in prison in this insane world of the Nazis. But not Betsie, not even among Nazis.

Suddenly one day the door opened and the woman guard growled, "Here's a present for you, Jew-lover!" And she thrust a woman into the cell.

Corrie had a cellmate!

But the woman seemed in the depths of despair. Corrie put her arm around her. "Cheer up. We'll keep each other great company."

The woman looked at her with red-rimmed eyes. "I'm going to be executed."

"Surely not!" How could the woman know for sure? No one seemed to know anything for sure here in prison. Corrie didn't even know her own sentence. Probably a vicious anti-Semitic guard had said that to frighten the poor woman out of her wits. "I'm sure it's not true," consoled Corrie.

But the woman was inconsolable. She insisted she had been sentenced to death. Eventually Corrie found out the woman's name was Helen, and she came to believe the woman's fear. Corrie even offered her Jesus for comfort. She had never done that to the Jews hiding in the Beje. Because they were being persecuted for being Jews it seemed to the ten Booms that it was wrong to evangelize. But if Helen was going to die, Corrie felt she could find comfort in Jesus. And more important, salvation.

Helen prayed, but it was either in self-pity or anger. According to Helen, she had no sin. She was faultless. In her saner moments, she reminisced about her wealth and how if she had managed things better she would have been wealthier yet. Corrie found her heart turning cold to Helen. Suddenly, one morning, Helen was lead out by a guard and a soldier.

"Where is she going?" yelled Corrie. "Her hat and coat are still here."

Not long after Helen left the cell, Corrie was allowed to exercise in an open area inside the prison. Other prisoners walked there, too. Corrie could smell the North Sea beyond the wall. Her rubbery legs walked a rectangular path around a lawn. Shrubs by the path flowered red. Primroses were in bloom. The sun was warm. The sky was blue. Was this so bad? Surely she could endure this. Did monsters keep such gardens as this?

But then she saw a freshly dug trench. No. She must not even think her suspicions. But it spoiled her reverie. She noticed now the high walls were topped with broken glass. There was a burning smell in the air, too. It smelled like nothing she had ever smelled before. Her soul wanted to cry out. Another inmate walked by her and whispered the smell was from burning flesh. The prison has a crematorium. *No! That is too preposterous,* thought Corrie. Not even Nazis are that evil. Suddenly her ears were pounded by noises beyond the walls. Is that a jackhammer? She was afraid to look at the other inmate.

THERE WAS A BURNING SMELL IN THE AIR. IT SMELLED LIKE NOTHING SHE HAD EVER SMELLED BEFORE.

"That was a machine gun," whispered the inmate. "I know. I was at Rotterdam."

Corrie welcomed her gray cell. *Oh Lord, let me out only when I can walk with children of the light.* Helen was not back. But her hat and coat were gone.

It was only days later that Corrie listened to rain fall outside her window. It was a gray, gloomy day when one wanted nothing to happen. What good could happen on such a gloomy day? She chided herself. Now she was letting the weather be her Ouija board. She heard the footsteps of a guard. *Just keep right on walking,* prayed Corrie.

She heard a key in the lock. The door opened and a woman guard stepped inside. "Come with me, ten Boom."

Corrie asked, "Do I need my coat and hat?"

"No!" The guard raised her billy club. "Do as I say! Come with me. Stay off the mat!"

12.
LIEUTENANT RAHM

The guard led Corrie into a courtyard somewhere in the midst of the prison. In the courtyard were four small huts. The guard knocked on the door of one hut. Corrie stood beside her, rain dripping down her face.

After a voice inside answered, the guard pushed Corrie inside. A tall, thin man in a crisp gray-and-black uniform of the Nazis stood by a small potbellied stove. "I'm Lieutenant Rahm," he said in Dutch. "Sit down. It's chilly in here," he added, more to himself than Corrie.

Corrie sat. The chair had a back and arms. She felt so privileged. She watched the lieutenant scoop coal into the stove. He was in no hurry. She enjoyed every minute of the experience. Did he know that? Was that why he dawdled, stirring the coals around with a poker? How could she credit a Nazi with such feelings of compassion? But soon he had a cozy fire started. She smelled and felt the warmth. What luxury.

He sat down. "If I'm going to help you, you must tell me everything."

So that was it. The snake was just getting her to relax. "What would you like to know?" she asked dully.

Lieutenant Rahm discretely probed. His face was chiseled with sharp features, a face easy to interpret as evil. Yet the face had something soft and haunting, too. Corrie had seen that look before. But she must not jump to conclusions with a Nazi. After many questions Corrie figured out what he was after. He had a list of people and addresses the Gestapo must have found at the Beje. It was a very real list of Dutch people active in the underground. But the lieutenant seemed to think the Beje might have been a center for planning raids on food offices and stealing food ration books. He seemed unable to make sense of the list. No one could ever make sense of the list from the Beje in regard to raids on food offices. Corrie relaxed, blissful in her ignorance. She could betray no one in any operations that raided food offices.

"I don't know what you mean," she kept repeating.

All the while she enumerated her many activities before the occupation. Yes, she took teenaged girls hiking and camping. Yes, she helped raise children left in Holland by missionaries. Yes, she gave Sunday school lessons to disabled children.

> "I DON'T KNOW WHAT YOU MEAN," SHE KEPT REPEATING.

"Disabled children?" It was the first time his face looked hard like the Nazi he was. "What a terrible waste."

"God values a disabled child as much as a watchmaker like me." *And more than a lieutenant like you,* she thought to herself.

"And just how do you know what God thinks?" he asked. His eyes were sorrowful.

"He gave us the Bible, so we would know what He thinks."

The lieutenant sighed. "I believe we have talked enough." He looked at his notepad. He had written nothing but doodles. He rose and opened the door. "Guard, take the prisoner back to her cell."

Next day Corrie was back. This time the lieutenant held their conference in the courtyard. They sat by a wall. "You need sun," he said. During a long pause Corrie closed her eyes and honored the sun. Finally he said, "I couldn't sleep last night. I kept thinking about the work I do. And I kept thinking about the work you used to do before we came here to Holland."

"Are you worried?"

"My wife and children are in Bremen. Bremen is being bombed. The war is going very badly."

This time she was sure about the look in his face. Corrie had not counseled hundreds of young people out of their despair without knowing all the symptoms of someone truly crying out for God. "You are in darkness, lieutenant."

"A good person like you cannot know darkness like mine."

"Jesus is the light of the world. Whoever follows Jesus will never walk in darkness." Did this man know the words of Jesus in the book of John? No, the lieutenant showed no trace of recognition.

Corrie told him the story of her life. He couldn't believe such a righteous family existed. He asked again and again to hear about Papa and Mama and Aunt Jans and Aunt Anna. His curiosity was insatiable. Finally she knew he believed her.

"If only I could raise my own family that way," he lamented.

"There is always a second chance with Jesus. It's never too late."

THE LIEUTENANT FED THE FLAMES WITH THE LIST OF ALL THE NAMES OF THOSE DUTCH PEOPLE IN THE UNDERGROUND.

She had four hearings with the lieutenant. She learned a little about her own situation. Her solitary confinement was not punishment. She was isolated because of her contagious illness. She was in prison, specifically charged with helping Jews. But for how long she could not discover.

In one session when the lieutenant's hut had not the slightest chill, the lieutenant stoked up a fire in the small stove. Then he took a file folder from his desk and stood by the stove. Corrie could see it was her file. He fed the flames with the list of all the names of those Dutch people in the underground—a list a diligent Gestapo officer could have used to make arrest after arrest whether he could prove anything or not. Her file thinned to almost nothing as paper after paper disappeared in flames.

"I believe we are warm enough now," he said. "I have a paper for you to sign. It's a deposition summarizing your knowledge of the Dutch underground. But I have seldom met a person more ignorant of the underground than you."

It was the first week in June when she was escorted to the lieutenant's office again. Inside was Nollie! And Betsie! And Willem! Tine and Flip!

"We are being released!" cried Corrie and wildly hugged them.

"No," said Betsie, hanging tight to Corrie. "It's the reading of Papa's will."

The lieutenant excused himself. He looked haggard and haunted as he walked outside. When the door closed Willem said, "Everyone thinks the invasion is coming! Pray to God that the British and Americans are soon headed this way. The Russians are already rolling over the Germans from the other direction. Praise God, the Nazis are almost finished."

They discussed what they knew about Papa's death, which was nothing more than that he had died in the corridor of a hospital waiting for treatment. He could have suffered far more. While they talked Nollie pressed a pouch in Corrie's hand. It contained a complete Bible! Corrie quickly put the string of the pouch over her head and slipped the treasure down inside her dress. Willem believed they might get Corrie transferred to a sanitarium because of her illness. The paperwork was being done.

Suddenly the lieutenant returned to read the will. He had left them alone as long as he could. The will surprised no one. There was no money, only the Beje. And Papa left it to shelter Corrie and Betsie as long as they wished.

Willem prayed, "Lord Jesus, we thank You for bringing us together for a while. Take this good man, Lieutenant Rahm, and his family into your constant care. Amen." The lieutenant's face came alive with hope.

Parting with her family would have weighed Corrie down if the prison had not erupted a few days after that. After the morning meal, guards were screaming everywhere. "Inmates must throw their belongings into pillow slips and stand at attention in the hallways!" they yelled.

After a tiresome wait in the hallway, Corrie heard the guards scream, "March this way!" They didn't even bother to mention the precious mats.

In the courtyard next to the outside gate were buses! Corrie searched desperately for Betsie. Maybe they could get together at last. But Betsie was nowhere to be seen in the milling prisoners. *Oh please, Jesus, let us be together again,* prayed Corrie, as the buses spewed black smoke and churned across the countryside.

When the buses unloaded them at the railway station, they stood at attention once again until their legs were shaky. Suddenly they were streaming onto railroad cars. Corrie hung back. Where was Betsie? *Oh please, God, let us be together through this.* As she was jostled along toward a railroad car, she saw Betsie behind her. Her prayer was answered! She waited and threw her arms around her. They were giddy as they found seats together on the car. How she had missed Betsie. Oh, how Betsie could make any suffering joyous!

"The British and Americans must be on their way," said Betsie.

"Is that why we are being moved?" Corrie shook her head. "And still the Nazis worry about small fry like us. Praise the Lord the devils are such fools."

The sisters talked for hours, loud at first like everyone else, but finally in hushed whispers. Corrie was stunned to hear that Betsie had prayed with Lieutenant Rahm, too. So sweet Betsie had something to do with his remorse, too. Corrie should have known.

"Thank the Lord we Dutch do not have an evil government," said Betsie. "You know, Corrie, many Germans are victims of the Nazi madness, too." And they both prayed for the lieutenant and his family.

CORRIE WAS STUNNED TO HEAR THAT BETSIE HAD PRAYED WITH LIEUTENANT RAHM, TOO.

"We must try to stay together," said Corrie. What happiness to be with Betsie again!

"Praise to God that we are not going east to Germany," whispered Betsie. "A while ago I thought I saw in the distance the cathedral in Delft."

"If you're right, we're going south." Corrie was so happy to be with Betsie she had not worried where they were headed. Betsie didn't really worry at all. Betsie was certain every action was planned by God, no matter how hard it was for a human mind to understand. But Corrie wasn't at all sure of that. Now she was worried. Before she went to prison, she really did not believe the terrible stories about death camps in Germany. But how could she doubt them now?

Corrie pressed her face against the glass. "If only the clouds would part for a moment." If only she could see the stars. How many hours had she gazed at the night sky with her club girls?

She sat on the left side of the train. If she saw the golden warmth of the star Arcturus, they were headed north, deeper into Holland. If she saw that icy blue diamond Vega, they were headed south toward Belgium. But if she saw the north star—God forbid—they were headed east into hell: Germany. *Please God, don't let it be the northern sky I see,* she prayed.

For just a moment Corrie thought she saw Vega! They were headed south! Should she tell Betsie? Not yet. The wheels changed pitch. The train was zipping across a trestle. But the trestle went on and on. Only one bridge was that wide. The bridge at Moerdijk. They were headed south!

She turned to Betsie. "We're headed—"

"South," said Betsie.

They hugged each other and thanked God.

Sometime in the night they stopped. They were rudely prodded off the train. Soldiers brandishing rifles bordered a rough path through the woods. The prisoners stumbled through the night. They slogged through puddles where it had rained. A soldier brutally kicked a woman who wandered off the path to avoid a puddle. Corrie and Betsie winced and struggled on. *Oh, how malleable people are,* thought Corrie. *We prisoners have no idea how long this nightmare will continue, yet we labor on obediently, almost complacent, no reward except that we avoid as much abuse as possible. We are still alive.*

They learned during the next day that they were in Holland on the perimeter of a prison camp near the village of Vught. This was not a Dutch prison. It was a concentration camp built by the Nazis for political prisoners. That fact was enough to alert everyone that this camp might not be an improvement over Scheveningen. For days the newcomers were idle as they were being processed into the camp.

"It seems the Nazis were not quite prepared for all the inconveniences of an invasion," said one newcomer bitterly.

But one day Corrie and Betsie were prodded into a long line. The news filtered back down the line: twenty women at a time were being herded into a shower. Finally as the two sisters neared the head of the line they heard a guard shout "Undress!" His voice was nasty, but there was more in it. Soon they could see the men guards relishing their power, laughing as they enjoyed the sight of naked women wiggling under the icy water. The women had to shower right out in the open!

Oh please, God, don't make us do this, prayed Corrie as she and Betsie waited in a long line of women. *Poor, sweet, innocent Betsie. Don't let this happen to her, Lord.*

Moments before their group was to undress, a guard yelled, "We are out of uniforms. Send the cows back later." His voice was bored. How much flesh can even corrupt Nazi eyes absorb?

When the women's camp received a new supply of uniforms, the men guards had returned to the men's camp. Corrie and Betsie showered under the sneering eyes of women guards. It was degrading but still a small miracle.

"Praise the Lord," said Betsie.

In their barracks lived 150 women. And small children! It seemed so strange to be around children again. If a new prisoner was pregnant, she had her child in the camp, and there the child remained. The inmates slept on real beds with two blankets. The ten Boom sisters must have looked warmhearted. Corrie knew Betsie did; she radiated love. A young Jewish girl walked right up to her like a baby chick. "I'm so scared." And Betsie pulled her into her arms.

There was an undercurrent of joy in most prisoners. Camp life really was better than prison life. The British and Americans were coming. It was inevitable now. The prisoners were sure. Corrie didn't even mind wearing a uniform of blue overalls with a

> THERE WAS AN UNDERCURRENT OF JOY IN MOST PRISONERS. CAMP LIFE REALLY WAS BETTER THAN PRISON LIFE.

red stripe down each leg. Her own clothes were rotting after three months of constant wear. But Corrie did mind the crude wooden clogs they were forced to clomp around in.

The Nazis were short of soldiers. Work was largely in the hands of prisoners. An *oberkapo*, or boss, a prisoner himself, examined the newcomers, as icy-veined as any Nazi. How power corrupts! Frail Betsie did not fool the oberkapo. He contemptuously shunted her aside into a group of the infirm who sewed prison uniforms. Corrie was marched to the "Phillips factory," which was no more than additional barracks situated between the women's camp and the men's camp. Hundreds of men and women prisoners sat on benches hunched over radio parts on long tables. Guards rarely strolled the aisles. The work was supervised by another oberkapo, a very soft-spoken, very shrewd Dutchman named Moorman.

He soothed even the Nazis. "We can increase production substantially more, Captain," he would say in the monotone of a good, colorless engineer, "at no sacrifice to quality."

But as soon as the Nazis were gone, the barracks exploded with laughter. After grim Scheveningen, Corrie couldn't believe such high spirits. Was this one of the notorious Nazi work camps? It was hot in the barracks in summer. Corrie rolled up her pant legs. A girl suddenly flung a mug of water on Moorman. He retaliated. The tables were soaked. No one cared. Soon the others carried both of the water-throwers into the bathroom. The girl was held in a large industrial sink, squirming and laughing under the gushing faucets.

"This is quite an unusual 'factory,'" said Corrie.

With Corrie's energy and background, she was soon assembling radios instead of sorting parts as they arrived. The real art was to assemble the radio in such a way that it was hopelessly defective but not obviously defective. The radios were installed in German fighter planes. More than once Corrie woke from a nightmare in which a German pilot was screaming into a dead radio that a fellow pilot had a Spitfire on his tail, just before the Messerschmidt was blasted out of the sky! She didn't tell Betsie what she was doing. Oh, how the Nazis corrupted!

The undermanned Nazis did reward the workers for their twelve-hour workday. Here at Vught they ate three times a day. And the food was better than the food at Scheveningen. After lunch the workers even had an hour off to rest. It was summer, so Corrie would stretch out on the ground for a nap. There was plenty of time for chatter while they worked—if no guards were strolling the aisles.

One day a voice woke her. "Corrie?"

Corrie blinked the sleep out of her eyes. "Mien? What joy!"

Mien van Dantzig also worked in the Phillips factory—the very sister of Hennie who had worked in the watch shop in the Beje. Mien was a thin young woman and very sly. Corrie soon learned she was a "scrounger." She helped the nurse in the camp. If a prisoner needed medicine Mien might be able to get it for them.

Betsie greeted Corrie every evening at the barracks. She would say warm things to Corrie, such as, "I prayed with a woman from Hilversum today who knows Willem," or chilling things, such as, "A Belgian woman just got here who said the British and Americans are trapped at Cherbourg," or cheering things, such as, "The Russians are in Poland already!"

Their talk transcended gossip. To survive, one listened to

information, judged its credibility, and shared it with others. She and Betsie even found out the name of their betrayer! He was a Dutchman from Ermelo. How Corrie hated him. And how she hated herself for hating him. Jesus commanded her to forgive enemies. But how could she ever forgive the wretch who caused Papa to die? And to think what suffering she and Betsie had been through! Betsie was weaker every day. And Willem had looked very unhealthy when she saw him in Lieutenant Rahm's office.

> SHE AND BETSIE FOUND OUT THE NAME OF THEIR BETRAYER! HOW CORRIE HATED HIM. AND HOW SHE HATED HERSELF FOR HATING HIM.

One night she argued about it with Betsie. Betsie had forgiven the traitor, even prayed for him!

"Pray for that devil? Never!" said Corrie.

"Think how much he must hate himself," answered Betsie. "Think how much he is suffering."

Corrie was skeptical but Betsie prevailed. Corrie forced herself to pray for him, too. She knew from years of trying to live in Christ that a righteous act, no matter how reluctantly performed, often captured the heart. But she doubted it would work in the case of this dreadful traitor. But praying did do something for her. For the first time since she learned the man's identity, Corrie slept without bitterness and anger.

The prison routine rarely varied. Stiff and sore, Corrie stumbled out for first roll call at five o'clock. She ate black bread and drank blacker coffee at five-thirty. She hiked to the Phillips factory where she worked until six o'clock in the evening. She trudged back to spend precious free time with Betsie. She kept telling herself that a

Christian can never really be imprisoned.

They were allowed to exchange letters again with Nollie's family and Willem's family. Nollie's first letter to Corrie got them very excited. Corrie could scarcely believe her eyes.

13.
HELL ON EARTH

Nollie's letter to Corrie read:

> *Oh, my dear child, how I am longing for you. . . . After we were together in Scheveningen, the notary and a few others went to see the gentlemen who are now in charge of your case, and the result was that the house and the shop were released. We went there immediately and cleaned the whole house. The shop is open and everything is waiting for you both. We have been absolutely assured that the letter for your release was sent some time ago. . . . Mr. Rahm phoned again to say that the letter, which will set you free, has been sent.*

Hallelujah! Freedom!

Was it possible? Corrie and Betsie were breathless as they motioned a gnarled veteran named Floor to meet them in the latrine. All important business took place in the latrine. The men guards, as brutal as they were, never went there. A lookout was posted to watch out for the women guards.

In the latrine the veteran Floor told the sisters, "If you helped Jews that gets you locked up for six months."

"Are you sure?" asked Corrie.

"You know the Germans. If that is what it says in their little Nazi rule book that is what it is. You'd have to get that crackpot Hitler to change one of his own rules."

"Six months?" cried Corrie. "Let me see. We started our sentence the last day of February. March, April, May, June, July, August. We'll be free by September 1st!"

Corrie and Betsie rejoiced. Less than two months to go! They could serve that time easily. They gave Bible lessons to the others. They sang hymns. They gave evening devotions. As more time passed they began to give sermons. Several dozen inmates, putting their bitterness on hold, listened to the ten Boom sisters deliver the gospel.

Corrie had gained twenty pounds in the camp! She could almost have become complacent if she weren't so worried about Betsie. Poor Betsie weighed less than one hundred pounds. Her glasses were always broken, always askew. She had to pin her overall straps closer together to keep her modesty. Even packages from Nollie crammed with sausages and fudge couldn't seem to keep Betsie from wasting away. And Corrie discovered the sewing brigade wasn't such a wonderful thing. Many times the brigade had to braid rope, and at the end of the day Betsie's long delicate hands were raw and bleeding. Corrie knew if there was one thing an anemic person couldn't withstand very long it was bleeding.

To squelch the last crumb of complacency Corrie might have harbored, there was the men's camp next to the women's camp. Every rifle shot ringing from the men's camp brought

> EVERY RIFLE SHOT RINGING FROM THE MEN'S CAMP BROUGHT SUSPICIONS OF AN EXECUTION.

suspicions of an execution. At first she and Betsie refused to believe executions were so routine. It was too monstrous. But Corrie worked at the Phillips factory with men from the camp next to them. And many of the women had husbands in the camp.

"No," insisted one worried wife. "Executions are not just rumors. They are real."

Grief hung over the women's camp—always. If things weren't gloomy enough, Mien had a nervous breakdown. Who knew what had happened to the sly scrounger? Corrie had worried about her. She thought Mien was sinking. Mien never got packages from home like the others. Corrie implored Nollie in her letters to ask Hennie to send Mien food and clothes. The packages meant so much more that. They meant someone was out there who cared. But Mien never got a package. When she came down with the flu the fever robbed all her remaining courage. She fell apart.

Corrie took her under her wing. "How can we ever thank you for all your help, Mien?" She told Mien the same thing Papa always told his children in the Beje, all fifteen of them. "It is time to lay your burden on Jesus. When Jesus takes your hand, He holds it tight. When He holds you tight, He leads you through your whole life. When Jesus leads you through your life, He brings you safely home. Mien, you are now under the constant care of Jesus, no matter what happens."

Mien began to recover.

How Corrie longed for September 1st and freedom! Miracles did happen in the camp. Betsie was inmate number 1130 and Corrie 1131. One morning at roll call when the cold-blooded matron called someone who was to be released, her voice choked. She gasped, "Inmate number one!"

The very first woman inmate of the camp lurched forward from the ranks, in a daze. As the others marched off to work the poor woman slumped on a bench. How many years had she been there? What "crime" had she committed against the glorious Third Reich? Praise to God, she was free at last.

And then came the best rumor yet: The British and Americans had taken Paris back! Their ground forces were knifing through France. They would soon cut Hitler's throat! Could it be true? Soon they saw proof with their own eyes. Almost daily by the end of August hundreds of silvery planes glimmered overhead, all headed east into Germany. One afternoon after the great silvery armada passed overhead, the women heard what must have been a tremendous battle in the sky just east of them. They laughed like fools as projectiles nicked trees around them and pinged into the barracks. Corrie later learned five women were in the hospital, injured by shrapnel.

Days later, explosions rocked the area.

"Bombs?" asked Corrie at the Phillips factory.

"No," said Moorman, "The Nazis are blowing up all the bridges." She had never seen him so serious. Oh, he was a wonderful actor around the Nazis. But something else was in his face. A deep worry.

"What do you suppose it is?" Corrie asked Betsie later.

"I don't know. Let's find Floor."

Floor turned their blood to ice. "They're blowing up the bridges here. These Nazis are going to pull out and blow up every bridge between here and Germany. The question is: What are they going to do with us? Take us with them? Or leave us here? And if they do leave us here, is it with a song of freedom on our lips—or rotting in a mass grave? Which do you think Nazis will do?" She sounded very bitter.

"Surely they won't execute the whole camp?" said Betsie in horror.

"Maybe not us. They don't respect us. They think we are weaklings. But I'm not so sure about the men."

Corrie was stunned. For a hundred reasons. She could only say, "But our time is almost up."

Floor laughed sourly. "Do you think they're going to process anyone for release now?" And she continued as if speaking just to herself, "Winter is a very bad time in the camps. And this winter will be the worst yet. No fuel. Little food. The weak ones will never..." She seemed to notice Betsie. "Never mind. Enough of this doomsday talk."

Corrie said unconvincingly, "She's wrong, Betsie. We'll be free on September 1st."

As the magic date approached, conditions worsened in the camps. Executions in the men's camp were more frequent. Guards were extremely edgy in the women's camp. The women guards even got ugly with the prostitutes, who were usually immune to any kind of punishment. The prostitutes were protected by the men guards. The women guards despised the prostitutes but feared the men guards more. It was the prostitutes who strolled out of the barracks late to roll call, who violated the boundaries of the camp, who lolled about, who sassed any woman guard any time they felt like it. But now they were being harassed by the women guards. That new attitude frightened the other women. It didn't take Sherlock Holmes to figure out that the women guards knew the exalted status of the prostitutes was about to end. And that was not good news for the other women either.

PRISONERS WHO GAVE UP HOPE SEEMED TO HAVE TERRIBLE ACCIDENTS.

Finally the day arrived: September 1! It was a Friday. Corrie could hardly wait through morning roll call to hear the list of prisoners to be released. But there was no list that day. She stumbled off to the Phillips factory, as depressed as she had been at any time since she arrived in the camp. How she had waited for this day! She forced herself to be more alert. She prayed to Jesus for courage. Where else would she get it? She had to have it. This was a dangerous time. Prisoners who gave up hope seemed to have terrible accidents.

That night Betsie consoled her, "The notice of our release may be a day or two late. The Nazis seem to be distracted now."

Sweet Betsie. Who was more vulnerable than she was? And yet she had to console Corrie. Corrie was ashamed. But she did have a feeling of dread. They had to get their freedom now. If they didn't, two terrible choices awaited them: execution here or winter in Germany.

After another two days Betsie admitted, "Maybe they started our sentence when we arrived here at the camp. What would that make our release date?"

Corrie figured furiously. "December 9!" she said, not so triumphantly. Where would they be then? Every night now she prayed for God's help more desperately. The madness of the Nazis was overwhelming her. Oh, the injustice. What if they were taken to Germany at the last moment before their release? What if they were executed? The terrible injustice. Only Christ's suffering—so much worse than her own—kept her from giving up.

Rumors oozed through the camps now: The British and Americans had captured Brussels. Belgium was almost free again. Holland would soon be free! No. Brussels was still in the clutches of the Nazis. No, the British and Americans had Brussels, but they were going to bypass Holland and thrust straight to the black heart of Germany. No, the British and Americans were going to free Holland first.

They would take each rumor and extrapolate. The latrine was crowded with orators. If Holland was bypassed, their life would not change that much. No, in that case the guards would take it out on the prisoners. If Holland was attacked, they would be executed; the Nazis had no time for prisoners. No, they would be evacuated to Germany; Hitler was a madman bent on revenge. No, they would be freed. The Nazis wanted leniency after they lost the war. On and on went the arguments.

If there was one thing Corrie knew, it was that their captors knew as little as their captives. Everyone in Holland knew something about how Nazis suppressed the truth and advanced their lies—even to their own stooges.

One morning there was no roll call.

A guard burst into the barracks long after they were usually up. "Get your things together!" she screamed. The guard was frightened.

The women heard the dreaded *pop-pop-pop* of rifles from the men's camp. Were the men being executed? What was happening? Were the Americans and British attacking? Perhaps they parachuted during the night! The women were marched into a field. There, unbelievably, a German soldier stood in the bed of an Army truck passing out blankets. A thousand women filed past and took a blanket. But hadn't they just left blankets in the camp?

They marched out of the camp in their usual five abreast. As they passed through the gates, Corrie saw the same rough, wooded path they had walked three months ago. They marched to the same railroad tracks. Soldiers lined them up along the track three deep. They waited, clutching their blankets and pillowcases stuffed with belongings. They whispered excitedly. Were they going back the same way? Would they ride that same train back to The Hague? Praise the Lord.

Betsie grabbed Corrie's arm. "There is no passenger train here. Only a freight train."

Far down the track were men prisoners. Maybe there were no

executions. Who could know for sure? Some women were saying 180 had been shot. Some were saying 700. Some were saying none. Who could know the truth in the Nazi madness?

On top of the freight cars were German soldiers with machine guns. More soldiers were walking along side the train, stopping at each car, throwing the bolt lock then sliding the door open. After they opened the door to the car nearest Corrie, a red-faced soldier yelled, *"Schnell! Gehen sie weg!"*

The women were being forced inside the freight cars! The soldiers helped them climb up though the door, soon breathless from laughing and grabbing handfuls of unwilling flesh as the women scrambled awkwardly into the freight car. Corrie flailed at their steely groping fingers. She swatted their filthy hands off Betsie. The prettier the woman the more outrageously they pinched and groped her. But the worst treatment went to a Dutch woman with a red circle patched on the back of her overalls. That patch meant she had tried to escape from the camp. This woman had no protection at all. They slapped her to the ground and kicked her senseless before they picked her up and threw her in the boxcar. Somehow she still clutched her pillowcase and blanket.

A soldier growled at her in German, "Good-bye, troublemaker. You will soon know what trouble is!"

The car stank of mildewed grain. The women were all standing up on the rough wooden floor of the car. But the soldiers kept adding women until they stood so close together Corrie had to wonder how they would ever rest. Suddenly they were plunged into blackness. The bolt slammed shut on the door. They were locked in!

> SUDDENLY THEY WERE PLUNGED INTO BLACKNESS. THE BOLT SLAMMED SHUT ON THE DOOR.

"Oh Jesus, save us," prayed Corrie.

"Thank God Papa is in heaven," said Betsie.

Somehow in the darkness they found rest. They sat like members of a bobsled team, their legs wrapped around the hips of the woman in front of them. Buffered by blankets it was almost tolerable. Those on the side were attacking the walls. They had to have air. With anything they could find they gouged tiny holes until sunlight appeared.

The train lurched ahead—its destination unknown to the inmates. When Corrie got her turn at an air hole she saw the night sky. She was on the right side of the train. There was Antares in the southern sky. They were traveling east—into Germany. She couldn't bring herself to tell Betsie. They were already in hell.

The air in the car was very foul. If there were buckets for waste in her part of the car, they knew nothing about them. Somewhere in the car bread was stored because it was being passed around. But the smell in the car was nauseating. It would be a long time before Corrie could eat her piece of bread in that stench. And she was very thirsty.

Each day the car got hotter and hotter.

Corrie prayed the ride was a nightmare few people would ever have to endure. They were numb with heat and thirst and the stench of soiled clothing. The sun was blinding when the door opened somewhere and a guard ordered them out.

They were too stiff to stand up and walk.

They crawled to the light and fell out the opening like blind crabs, clutching their blanket and pillowcase. They sprawled like fish on a bank gasping for air, praying for water. Yes, someone had a pail. There was a lake nearby, someone said. The stronger ones began to crawl toward the lake. Corrie stayed with Betsie. She made sure Betsie got water when pails of water finally worked their way back to the weak ones still sprawled by the tracks.

Corrie began to look around. Their guards were young boys in baggy uniforms, standing far off, repelled by the stinking women.

"Where are we?" yelled a woman in German.

"Furstenburg," replied a scowling boy.

"Furstenburg? Where is Furstenburg?" asked another woman.

"Southeast of Berlin, you stupid cow," snapped a boy.

"Thanks, you miserable brat," muttered the woman in Dutch. "What rat doesn't know where your famous village is located?"

Corrie looked at Betsie. Yes, she was pitying the boys. That was Betsie. She was merely seeing more victims of the Nazis. If Betsie had been strong enough she probably would have been on her feet organizing a prayer meeting among the boys. But she looked very old today, far older than her fifty-nine years. More white showed under her pupils than ever before. Her sunken chest was heaving. She had scarcely moved since Corrie tried to soften her fall from the freight car.

"Get up, you cows!" screamed the boy who was still mad because the women had not known of tiny Furstenburg's fame.

The boys marched them along the shore of the lake then up a hill. The men prisoners were nowhere to be seen. They passed a few farmers and their families on the way. The country folk were red-cheeked, dressed in feathered caps and lederhosen. Could such people live their wonderfully pure lives these days? It seemed impossible. It was Betsie who reminded Corrie their good fortune was an illusion. That family had probably lost a brother, an uncle, a son somewhere in the mud of Russia.

When the women reached the crest of the hill they saw down in the next valley their new camp. It was not a scar in the woods like Vught. This camp was a cancer, the trees having been cleared far back from the enclosure which was not wire fences but concrete walls with strands of wire at the top. Inside the walls stretched dozens and dozens of cold, gray barracks. A tall stack fouled the blue sky with smoke.

As they got closer, Corrie could see the strands strung along the top of the concrete walls were not barbed wire. ELECTRIFIED WIRE, warned the signs in German. Guard towers were spaced along the wall.

Corrie called to Floor, "What is this place?"

"Hell on earth." The blood seemed to have drained completely from Floor's face. "I think this must be Ravensbrück."

> ELECTRIFIED WIRE, WARNED THE SIGNS IN GERMAN.

14.
RAVENSBRÜCK

Betsie turned to Corrie, "Haven't we heard of Ravensbrück somewhere?"

"Yes," said Corrie numbly. "It's a work camp for women only."

Mien was suddenly there beside them. Her thin hand groped for Corrie's hand. "Is it true? Is this Ravensbrück?"

"Yes."

Any woman imprisoned in Holland by the Nazis had heard of Ravensbrück. Especially those women who had worked in the underground. Ravensbrück was not just a camp for women but a camp for women who were considered incorrigible by the Nazis. It was a work camp. But the rumor was that the inmates were worked to death. There was no way out. Ever.

"Oh Jesus, hold us tight," prayed Corrie.

Mien smiled bravely. A scrounger never gave up, especially when Jesus holds her tight. "It's not hopeless, Corrie. The Russians might bust through. They might overwhelm the camp at any moment. They couldn't be too far away, you know."

"You little dear," said Corrie. "You came to comfort Betsie and me, didn't you?"

And Corrie wondered how pitiful she must have looked. She knew Betsie looked bad. Her glasses were broken again. Nollie's blue sweater under her overalls draped on her like a bag. Her wrists looked as thin as sticks and as white as ivory.

Once inside the massive gates, dozens of guards drove the one thousand newcomers to a large tent. And there they waited day after day, often pointlessly standing at attention until their knees trembled. Ones who collapsed were taken away and not seen again. They were no longer under the tent but beside it in the open air. No one complained. They were veterans of Nazi inhumanity. It took the Nazis days and days to process prisoners. Besides, waiting must be better than working in this place. And anything was better than the hell of the freight cars.

"Oh please, Jesus," prayed Corrie, "don't let us suffer anything worse than the freight cars."

LICE AT RAVENSBRÜCK WERE NOT A NEW PROBLEM. IT WAS THEIR ABUNDANCE.

Lice at Ravensbrück were not a new problem. It was their abundance that was the problem. The ground swarmed with lice. The women had no choice. Their hair had to go. It was not the guards who insisted on it. The women did it themselves.

"Oh, Betsie, your beautiful chestnut hair," cried Corrie as she sheared the wavy locks off her sister. And it was more than that. Betsie looked so inconsequential with her tired, shorn head wobbling on a thin goose neck. Never had she looked so frail, so wispy, so marginally alive.

Betsie was silent as her hands snipped Corrie's hair. As the locks fell to the ground Corrie realized why. What could Betsie say? Corrie's thick dark blonde hair was now streaked white! Would anyone in Haarlem recognize her anymore? She could imagine one of her club girls walking up with a puzzled look, probably recognizing Corrie's knock-knees and pigeon toes, and saying "You look a lot like Corrie ten Boom, but of course she was a much younger woman."

"Why are you laughing?" asked Betsie.

"It's so much fun growing old in prison."

"Oh!" cried Betsie in real pain.

"What is wrong?"

"I have terrible cramps."

Corrie helped her sister to a ditch. How long could Betsie withstand diarrhea? She was a walking skeleton now.

They surrendered their names. Betsie was now Number 66729. Corrie was Number 66730. More of the reality of Ravensbrück soon hit them. They were asked to surrender all their belongings.

"But your own soldiers in Holland just gave us these blankets," protested one woman.

"Shut up!" A guard slapped the woman. "Apparently the soldiers who have been vacationing on the western front enjoy more luxuries than we do."

So, Corrie and Betsie speculated, the German soldiers fighting Russia were truly desperate. Why would they take secondhand blankets of prisoners otherwise? But Corrie was not gloating. She was fearful. Betsie needed Nollie's sweater. And the vitamins. And how could they live without their Bible?

The one thousand women lined up. The guards were shuttling fifty at a time into the shower room. Before they went into the shower room they dumped their possessions into a pile. No one seemed to be recording anything. It seemed painfully obvious nothing was going to be returned.

Farther on in the line the women stripped and dumped their clothing into a second pile. They then walked naked past several deadly serious guards into the shower. These guards were not leering.

They were tired of this place, of these emaciated, licey women. They hated it. When the women reappeared from the shower room each one wore a threadbare prison dress and leather shoes.

Before her group reached the first pile of abandoned possessions Corrie clutched the bottle of vitamins in her hand. Then she and Betsie dropped their blankets and pillow cases into the pile. How it hurt to surrender their nice blankets, combs, needles, thread, all the things they had so painstakingly collected over six months. But they still had their most precious possessions: vitamins, Betsie's sweater, and the Bible.

THEY STILL HAD THEIR MOST PRECIOUS POSSESSIONS: VITAMINS, BETSIE'S SWEATER, AND THE BIBLE.

Oh please, Jesus, prayed Corrie, *please allow us to keep Your precious Word.*

Suddenly Betsie doubled over, seized by a severe cramp.

"Please, sir," Corrie implored the guard in German, "she has diarrhea."

The guard scowled in disgust. "Well, don't let her do it here! Get her in there." He jabbed his finger at the shower room.

Corrie rushed Betsie into the shower room. No one was there. It was empty! They were between groups. Corrie quickly took the sweater from Betsie, wrapped the Bible and bottle of vitamins in the sweater and hid the bundle behind a wooden bench crawling with roaches. Stacked in the other end of the shower room were the dresses and shoes they were to wear.

They returned to the line, shed their Vught overalls, and Corrie imagined to herself no one saw them as they walked past the guards. Inside the shower room, after the short icy blast, they dressed in their new camp garb—plus one sweater, one bottle of vitamins, and one Bible. But their problems were not over. The Bible in the pouch hanging from Corrie's neck on a string was not well concealed under the flimsy dress. She had no choice but to pray again. *Oh please, Jesus, protect me. Surround me with your angels.*

They marched slowly past guards who made no effort to hide their disgust as they searched every woman from head to toe with groping hands. Rough hands covered the woman in front of Corrie. Rough hands covered Betsie behind Corrie. No hands touched Corrie. It was as if she were invisible. It seemed the worse things became for Corrie and Betsie, the more God intervened to protect them.

The one thousand newcomers spent day after day in Barracks 8, which was a quarantine compound. It was deliberately placed next to the barracks where women were punished. During the day the newcomers spent hours outside standing at attention. All day and all night they heard screams of agony. They heard whacks and thuds that caused the agony. Soon Corrie even flinched at silence. Silence meant the victim had either passed into pain so excruciating it was paralyzing or had died. It was heartrending to listen. Each day Corrie felt closer and closer to Jesus. How else could one endure such pain? She could never be defeated in Jesus.

"Jesus is Victor," said Betsie, who must have been thinking the same thoughts.

All the newcomers encouraged each other. Their permanent barracks would be better. They would have nice blankets again. They would get real medical attention when they needed it instead of degrading inspections every Friday in which they stripped naked to have their teeth examined. In their permanent barracks they wouldn't have to sleep five to a bed with one blanket. Gripers were shouted down in a hurry. No one was allowed to mention the obvious: Each night was colder.

One day Corrie heard a woman say, "I spent a couple of years in Germany when I was a girl."

"So what?" asked her neighbor suspiciously.

"I'll tell you why. Every night in January there is a hard freeze."

"It freezes in Holland, too."

"Not like here. Many nights here the temperature drops below zero."

Below zero! Was winter going to be that frigid?

Finally the guards marched them into the main camp and prodded them ten abreast past the permanent barracks. The small army would stop while several numbers were called, thinning their ranks, then continue. Corrie and Betsie stopped at Barracks 28. A not-very-happy guard briskly led them and several other newcomers, including Mien, straight into the dormitory.

"What a smell!" blurted Betsie.

"Ignore it, you cow," growled the guard. "There are worse things than that in here."

Perhaps one could learn to ignore the smell of rotting straw. Could one ignore the smell of vomit and human waste? But there were things that were worse. Their five to a bed seemed a wonderful luxury now. This dormitory was jammed with square platforms covered by straw and stacked three deep. The platforms were shoved together so that one aisle had to serve many platforms. Corrie and Betsie would have to crawl across three platforms to reach their own platform. What Corrie and Betsie did not know yet was how many women shared each platform square.

The guard quickly took the newcomers to a central room. About two hundred women were seated around tables, knitting Army socks from gray wool. "Get to work," said the guard, who no longer seemed to be in a hurry. Half a dozen other guards moved listlessly around the room.

Corrie and Betsie sat down. Corrie whispered in German to a woman next to her, "Is this a knitting barracks?"

"No. The others are out working."

"How many live here?"

"Fourteen hundred. The barracks are supposed to hold four hundred."

Corrie learned prisoners were from all over Europe. At first the camp had been full of Poles, Finns, and Russians. Now women flooded in from everywhere as the Nazis were being pushed back on all fronts. The barracks had Dutch, French, Belgians, Danes, Norwegians, and even some poor mysterious women no one in the barracks could communicate with at all.

PRISONERS FLOODED IN FROM EVERYWHERE AS THE NAZIS WERE BEING PUSHED BACK ON ALL FRONTS.

"And how many are in the camp?" asked Corrie of the woman.

"They say thirty-five thousand," she answered lifelessly.

The others returned at six o'clock from their work. But the last thing they wanted to talk about was work. And Corrie found little conversation from anyone but Betsie as they drank a tasteless broth with shreds of cabbage floating in it. After supper, once again they went outside to stand at roll call.

That night they learned more stark truths. Their half of the dormitory had eight toilets for seven hundred women. They shared the platform with seven other women, who were not happy about their arrival. A crash nearby and screams and curses informed them the slats under the straw were very unstable. And they learned they shared the platform with more than seven other women.

"Fleas!" cried Corrie as she slapped at the source of the sting.

"Remember First Thessalonians?" asked Betsie.

"I feel like I know the New Testament by heart. Why?"

"Recite chapter five, verse eleven."

" 'Wherefore comfort yourselves together'. . .and something else, then something or other. I guess I can't recite it."

Betsie laughed. "I can do it because I read it this morning. And it struck me very forcefully. 'Wherefore comfort yourselves together, and edify one another, even as also ye do. And we beseech you, brethren, to know them which labour among you, and are over you in the Lord, and admonish you; And to esteem them very highly in love for their work's sake. And be at peace among yourselves. Now we exhort you, brethren, warn them that are unruly, comfort the feebleminded, support the weak, be patient toward all men. See that none render evil for evil unto any man; but ever follow that which is good, both among yourselves, and to all men. Rejoice evermore. Pray without ceasing. In every thing give thanks: for this is the will of God in Christ Jesus concerning you.' "

"It's beautiful."

"It says 'give thanks in all circumstances.' "

So that's what Betsie was getting at. "Am I supposed to give thanks for fleas?" she asked sarcastically.

"Yes."

"Shut up!" screamed someone. "You must be in the knitting brigade not to want to go to sleep."

Corrie fell asleep thanking God for fleas. She was awakened by a whistle. Choking dust filled the air as women scrambled off the platforms for black bread and coffee in the knitting room. Slowpokes found little left.

"What time is it?" asked Corrie, chewing the tough bread. "Didn't we just fall asleep?"

"Four o'clock. Same time it was at this time yesterday," grumbled someone.

At four-thirty, fourteen hundred women stood outside Barracks

28 under streetlights for roll call. To Corrie it represented a further decline of their fortunes. At Vught they had roll call at five o'clock. Since February 29, 1944, it always seemed to Corrie that life could not get worse. But under the Nazis she learned life always did get worse.

Amazingly, Corrie and Betsie marched with several thousand other women right out of the massive gates of the camp, across the barren area, and into the woods!

"We're going to the Siemens factory," grunted a woman to Corrie's obvious question.

"What do they make?"

"Not cotton balls," said one woman bitterly.

The work at the Siemens factory was backbreaking. It was one of the great iron and steel works of Germany. Corrie and Betsie had to push a handcart to a door at the factory where German civilians loaded it with heavy metal plates. The civilians refused to look at the prisoners. Then Corrie and Betsie threw their weak middle-aged bodies into the loaded cart to push it along a dock where they finally stopped it by a boxcar. They tried to get their breath as they helped load the plates into the boxcar.

At lunch each prisoner feasted on one boiled potato and a cup of broth. "Praise the Lord," said Betsie weakly. "I heard in the camp they get nothing for lunch."

Betsie could hardly walk the mile and a half back to camp, not that any prisoner wanted to return to camp, but guards were quick to lash out at stragglers. The guards were particularly brutal on the way back to camp. They wanted their day to end as quickly as possible.

After a dinner of turnip soup, Betsie recovered enough for the most important moments of the day. They found a light bulb in the dormitory and read from the Bible. The first night those who had come with them from Vught joined them, along with a few of the curious.

Corrie was worried. Wouldn't it attract a guard? But strangely, guards were almost never to be seen in the dormitory of Barracks 28. And stranger still, Betsie got stronger and stronger as they read. As the days passed, the reading seemed to be enough to get her through the next work day as she weakened every minute during work and then strengthened every minute at night.

The nightly readings attracted more and more listeners. It was no longer enough to read the Bible in Dutch. Corrie would translate the passage into German. Another woman would repeat it in Russian. Another in Danish. Another in French. And on and on went God's true Word in the world's stumbling tongues.

CORRIE WOULD TRANSLATE THE PASSAGE INTO GERMAN. ANOTHER IN DANISH. ANOTHER IN FRENCH.

One night Corrie asked a woman, "Why do the guards never come in the dormitory?"

"They are repelled by the fleas."

"Praise the Lord for the fleas." And this time Corrie was more sincere. She was not proud of doubting God's Word. Another miraculous thing that happened to them was the miracle of the vitamin bottle. It never seemed to run out of drops of liquid. Corrie was just certain it had to be exhausted. But it wasn't. She fretted about it all the time. Betsie depended on the vitamins to fight her anemia. And to worry Corrie even more, Betsie shared the bottle with everyone who asked.

Betsie just shrugged. "Don't you remember in 1 Kings the story of Elijah and the widow of Zarephath of Sidon?"

Corrie blinked. "The widow who had the jar of flour and the jug of oil? And they both seemed almost empty, yet never ran out." But Corrie worried anyway. If only she had Betsie's faith. Nollie was like Betsie. Why was Corrie such a doubter? She remembered the man's cry for faith in chapter nine of Mark: "I believe; help thou mine unbelief!" That was her. *Oh God, help me believe,* she prayed.

One day Mien found Corrie. "Tonight you can relax," said Mien. She pressed something into Corrie's hand. It was a new bottle of vitamins! Once again wonderful little Mien had somehow attached herself to a nurse and was scrounging things for the inmates.

And that very night the old bottle of vitamins ran out of drops. It was bone dry.

Did God's miracles never cease? "Oh God, I do believe," said Corrie.

In November they were issued coats. And no more work details went to the Siemens factory. Why the work there stopped was a mystery. But bombs were dropping in the vicinity every night and the great iron and steel works was probably a prime target. And Ravensbrück was not that far from the most prime target of all: Berlin, the heart of the Third Reich—if such a monstrosity had a heart.

In the camp, Corrie and Betsie were put to work leveling rough ground close to the concrete wall. Shoveling dirt was grueling on the best of days. But this day was after a rain, and Corrie felt like she was shoveling lead instead of water-soaked soil. Betsie's health was failing. She could hardly lift her shovel. Corrie eyed the guard. Would the guard notice how little Betsie was doing?

Suddenly the guard was staring at Betsie!

15.
"CORRIE TEN BOOM, FALL OUT!"

Why are you not working harder?" screamed the guard at Betsie. "That's nothing but a spoonful of dirt on your shovel."

"I'm sorry," Betsie answered good-naturedly, "but even spoonfuls add up."

If the other prisoners hadn't laughed, Betsie probably would have been all right. But no one swollen with pride can stand laughter. The guard struck Betsie with a leather crop. Betsie was bleeding. Her precious blood, of which she had so little, was streaming into the void. Corrie wanted to kill the guard. Betsie grabbed her hand. She saw the hatred in Corrie's face.

That night Betsie said, "Perhaps we will be released December 9th. That's six months after we entered Vught."

"Of course," agreed Corrie, hiding her disbelief.

Rain and cold worsened Betsie's health. She now coughed blood. Again and again Corrie supported Betsie while she escorted her to the infirmary. Again and again the effort was in vain. Only a fever of 104 degrees got medical attention. Sick call itself was unhealthy,

ONLY A FEVER OF 104 DEGREES GOT MEDICAL ATTENTION.

even dangerous. The women stood in line outside in the elements for hours before they were examined.

One day Betsie reached the threshold. Even though she was finally admitted to the infirmary Corrie couldn't be happy. A temperature of 104 degrees was too close to fatal. Yet Betsie had to get medicine and rest. Betsie disappeared within the infirmary. Corrie was alone. How she wanted to be at Betsie's bedside.

Corrie had learned in three months at Ravensbrück how to disappear. The guards simply could not keep track of thirty-five thousand women. After Betsie had been in the infirmary two days, Corrie simply walked away from roll call to disappear into the morning fog.

Resourceful Mien had shown her a way to sneak into the hospital. Corrie went to an open window and crawled inside the latrine. It was so easy. This latrine was not one where inmates gathered to swap stories. This latrine held bodies of inmates of Ravensbrück who had died. Corrie picked her way through the corpses and went out the door.

She wandered the hallways peeking into wards until she found Betsie sitting on a cot.

"Betsie!" she cried.

"Yes, nurse?" answered Betsie. "Are you crazy?" Betsie mouthed silently as she glanced around the ward nervously. That was Betsie, never worried about herself but frantic over Corrie.

Corrie pretended to look at a clipboard. "You are looking much better, Number 66729. What did the doctor say?"

"I've never seen a doctor. But the relaxation is wonderful."

Corrie felt her forehead. It was hot. "Oh yes, you're much better. But you had better stay as long as you can, Number 66729." And in a whisper she added, "Praise the Lord, they're so slow."

Betsie returned to Barracks 28 three days later. No doctor had ever seen her. No medicine had ever been given to her. She still had a fever. But the visit was not in vain. She was rested. And somehow she had been transferred to the knitting room. Had Mien done something? The scrounger was everywhere. Her experience in the underground served her well. She kept her secrets to herself.

Corrie thought of Willem's son Kik. It seemed so many years ago he had said to her, "You must not ask questions. The less you know, the less the Gestapo can torture out of you." Not to mention the accidental betrayal. It would not be Corrie whose loose lips betrayed Mien.

The general health of the women was so poor now the knitting brigade overflowed into the dormitories. The dormitory was paradise for Betsie. She was a very fast knitter and finished her quota of socks by noon. And because a guard rarely ventured into the dormitory, she could move among the knitting brigade with the gospel. What bliss for frail Betsie.

Miraculously, one day Corrie joined her. She had intentionally not joined a work crew that would have taken her away from Ravensbrück. She simply walked into the central room like she belonged there, grabbed a skein of gray wool, and joined the knitting brigade in the dormitory.

BETSIE BEGAN TO SPEAK OF A MISSION AFTER THE WAR. THEY WOULD HELP PEOPLE WARPED BY THE WAR FIND JESUS.

Betsie began to speak of a mission after the war. They would help poor people who were warped by the war find Jesus. There would be plenty of them. She and Corrie would live with them. But not at the Beje. It wasn't big enough for Betsie's vision. She had envisioned a mansion in Haarlem. She could even describe the inlaid wood of the golden floors and the manicured gardens that surrounded it. There was a gallery around a central hall. Bas-relief statues adorned the walls. There were tall, leaded windows, a gabled roof. Corrie was stunned by how vivid Betsie's vision was. It seemed Betsie was standing right there in Haarlem looking at it. Once again, she seemed prophetic. Betsie really seemed to be living in Christ.

Corrie was trying to get there. She seemed terribly flawed to herself. But wasn't that the first step to redemption and living in Christ? She hoped and prayed that it was. Because every day revealed a flaw. One night she did not want to share a blanket with a newcomer. One morning she maneuvered herself into the middle of their ten-by-ten formation for roll call, so she wouldn't get so cold near the edge. She hoarded the bottle of vitamins. Her Bible reading was becoming mechanical. She read the words with her head but not her heart. What was happening to her? The closer Betsie got to God, the more Corrie drifted away!

At least she knew she was straying. "Oh Jesus, help me. I'm sinking."

One December day a passage from Paul's second letter to the Corinthians fairly exploded in her face:

> *And lest I should be exalted above measure through the abundance of the revelations, there was given to me a thorn in the flesh, the messenger of Satan to buffet me, lest I should be exalted above measure. For this thing I besought the Lord thrice, that it might depart from me. And he said unto me, My grace is sufficient for thee: for my strength is made perfect in weakness. Most gladly therefore will I rather glory in my infirmities, that the power of Christ may rest upon me. Therefore I take pleasure in infirmities, in reproaches, in necessities, in persecutions, in distresses for Christ's sake: for when I am weak, then am I strong.*

Her mistake was in thinking she was in power. Jesus was in power. And the weaker she became, the stronger Christ became. She could see it so plainly in Betsie's case. And now her own case, too.

One morning as Corrie read the Bible to a group of knitters, she noticed the group seemed frozen. Someone was behind her. It must have been a woman guard. Corrie could feel the hammering hearts of the other inmates. But Corrie's new strength, which was from Christ and not from herself, compelled her to forge ahead. When she put down the Bible and started singing a hymn, the other inmates were really frightened. Now they had to make a choice. How could they deny to the guard their willingness to celebrate the gospel if they sang now? But Christ's strength was in them, too. And they did sing.

After they finished the hymn Corrie waited for the leather crop to slice agony across her back. But a voice behind her pleaded, "Sing another one, like that one."

Later Corrie found that guard alone, so she could tell her about Jesus. Corrie knew now even the guards still had a tiny trace of decency left. Even the guards could be salvaged if they could find Christ. Hadn't Paul held the coats of the villains who stoned Stephen? She and Betsie got bolder and bolder in Christ.

> EVEN THE GUARDS COULD BE SALVAGED IF THEY COULD FIND CHRIST.

As blessed as Betsie's life was in the dormitory she could not escape the dreaded roll calls twice a day. In December the air iced their bones, and all too frequently they were kept at roll call until prisoners started keeling over. Dear, wonderful Mien brought them newspapers to insulate themselves but Betsie was getting weaker. December 9 came and passed. They still hoped to be released.

One week before Christmas, Betsie could not move off the platform for morning roll call. Another prisoner helped Corrie carry Betsie to roll call. Betsie had to go there before she could go to sick call. But blocking the door to the outside was a ruthless woman guard called Snake. It was not many days before this morning that Snake had whipped a disabled girl mercilessly for soiling herself.

Snake looked at them. "Get her back inside."

They carried Betsie back to the platform. Then miraculously, orderlies appeared in a few minutes with a stretcher. Snake even stood by as Betsie was carried away to the infirmary. It was as if God had intervened to put His hand on Snake. Betsie had suffered enough.

Even as Betsie was carried away she enjoyed her vision. "Corrie, we must tell people what we have learned here about Christ."

Maybe this time Betsie would get the medicine she needed. Corrie wasn't going to rush to the infirmary. It might botch things. It seemed now that Betsie had friends, even among the very worst Nazi guards. But one dreary day at noon, Corrie could wait no longer. She didn't even know if Christmas had come yet or not. She slipped away from her work detail and crept around the infirmary until she found the window looking in on Betsie's ward. There was her dear Betsie on a cot. Corrie tapped on the pane.

Betsie opened her eyes, looking very tired, probably sedated. She tried to smile. She nodded "Yes" after Corrie mouthed, "Are you all right?"

Praise the Lord, Betsie was resting, out of the cold. She was fifty-nine years old, but she had never been strong. She had a miraculously productive life for someone who was virtually an invalid. But why was Corrie thinking such final thoughts? Betsie would recover. They would be freed. They would open their mission. She just knew it. After all, Betsie had a vision. And God didn't make mistakes.

The next day she sneaked back. Where was Betsie? On a cot was the corpse of an old woman, completely naked. She was pitifully thin. Yellow skin stretched over bone. Hair was matted. It was so sad. But where was Betsie? Was Betsie up and about all already? It seemed too much to ask. What was that by the cot? Nollie's sweater?

And the truth hammered her. The dead woman was Betsie!

She stumbled from the window and wandered in a daze. Betsie! Dead! How was it possible? Her dear, sweet, older sister whom she had seen almost every day of her life for fifty-two years. And now she was dead. She had just weakened, second by second, day after day, week after week, month after month, and slipped away to Jesus. If only they had been released September 1! Or even December 9, sweet Betsie would have lived. But what had Betsie told her when the terrible occupation began? "*There are no 'ifs' in God's world.*" But what of Betsie's vision? How could Corrie make sense of it now? Betsie was gone.

"Corrie! Come quick," urged a voice.

It was Mien. Mien held her arm, gently urging her back to the infirmary. She couldn't go back there again.

"Don't you know what happened?" asked Corrie numbly.

"You must see this." And Mien guided her to the window of the latrine.

"No. Not there," pleaded Corrie. "That is where they put the corpses. Don't you understand I already know?" How much could she bear? Pushy, stubborn, helpful little Mien. Corrie was too weak to fight her. She looked over the window sill.

The sight inside stunned her.

Betsie was transformed. No longer yellow but ivory. No longer with drab, matted hair but neat chestnut locks. No longer skeletal but wonderfully formed. Her face was serene, at perfect peace. And why not? She was with the Lord in heaven.

"Oh, thank You, Jesus," cried Corrie. And she let herself grieve. She was missing sweet Betsie, of course. But Betsie was not lost, but found.

It was Betsie's vision that troubled Corrie. Betsie was gone. To paradise, yes. But why had she told Corrie her vision so many times? Because it dawned on Corrie that she was not going to survive either. How many roll calls in icy wind could her aging body withstand? She had long ago lost the weight she gained at Vught. She was a bag of bones. How much punishment could one undernourished, bony body take?

> BETSIE WAS SERENE, AT PERFECT PEACE. SHE WAS WITH THE LORD IN HEAVEN.

January would be even worse. She remembered the woman's warning: zero degrees! Corrie felt like her blood was frozen slush now. The strong ones stomped their feet during roll call to keep from freezing. But eventually one became too weak—like sweet Betsie—to do that. Corrie saw how swollen her own legs and feet had become. Her shoes were ridiculous flaps of leather. It only took one small cold, which became a bad cold with drainage, which became raging pneumonia, which became a woman's last rattling breath.

"Jesus, help me," she prayed. "I must not give up hope." She must never think Betsie suffered such a long time in vain. Sweet Betsie had changed the lives of so many inmates. But what if none of the prisoners survived? What was the point? The point was, she reminded herself, to save them in Jesus and get them to heaven.

Corrie must not lose sight of Betsie's great victory—which was really the victory of Jesus.

One morning at roll call the guard called out, "Corrie ten Boom. Fall out!"

Not Number 66730! But Corrie ten Boom. What did it mean? She was no fool. Some of the older women did not die. They simply disappeared. It was a horror no one talked about. And inmates talked about almost everything. But not that smokestack. There was never the sound of gunshots. One wouldn't need a bullet to kill an inmate of Ravensbrück. They were so weak a sharp blow to the head would do it. Besides they only had to be unconscious before they were fed into the furnace. Could even the Nazis be that horrid? Surely they weren't taking inmates still alive and reducing them to ashes. Surely they couldn't do that. How could the Nazis get anyone even among themselves to perform such an act against God and His creations?

So after all the waiting and hoping, it was no comfort to Corrie to have her name called at morning roll call. And it was no comfort to remain behind like Corrie did as the others went on their work details. It was no comfort to get release papers like Corrie got later that day. The Nazis were such devils.

She smelled a trap when she was taken for a medical examination. A doctor who appeared not much older than a teenager said, "You have edema. You must be treated before you can leave here."

She couldn't deny her feet and ankles were horribly swollen. But she had never been more suspicious. She was taken to a ward with very unhealthy inmates. They too had been "released." This delay was no comfort. The Nazis were slow, bungling, ugly—but as certain as a great cancer. This ward might be no more than a holding area until the Nazis could work through their backlog of undesirables at the furnace.

The timing of her release—if it was that—nagged at her, too. Betsie had not been dead one week. Why couldn't she have lived? Never had Corrie's trust in God been tested more. This *was* God's plan for her and Betsie, she kept telling herself. And no one would have insisted that was true more emphatically than Betsie herself.

So she must not give up hope. She gave her Bible to an inmate she hoped would continue Betsie's good work. She could get another Bible in Holland. Holland! Could her release be true? Or was this a trick? She waited for her release, wondering if Holland was free yet. Her swelling had gone down considerably now that she no longer stood at roll calls. Why were they keeping her? And she had a horrifying thought: If she were released just as the Russians arrived, would she ever get back to Holland anyway? She would be behind the Russian army. But she must not think that way. There are no "ifs" in God's world.

COULD HER RELEASE BE TRUE? OR WAS THIS A TRICK?

Her heart was in her mouth the morning they marched her and several other older inmates away from the infirmary to a shed near the outskirts of the camp.

A guard sneered. "Step inside the dressing shed."

Was this to be her last moment on earth?

16.
HOME TO HAARLEM

Dressing shed?" asked Corrie. Her heart was in her mouth. Was this another Nazi trick?

"You heard me!" snapped the guard. "Get inside, you cow!"

Once again she put her trust in God and stepped into the unknown. Inside the shed, a guard actually issued Corrie some underwear, a wool skirt, a silk blouse, and shoes, none of it new, but to her it looked too nice to wear. She was given papers to sign that she agreed she had never been mistreated at Ravensbrück. So that was it. Some Nazis were already thinking about the consequences of the war. And this was "proof" of their innocence. She signed the paper anyway. Freedom was too close—if this was not a diabolical trick.

Remarkably, the guards produced an envelope with her Alpina watch, gold ring, and Dutch guilders. "What are you gawking at?" snapped one of the guards.

Corrie answered, "I was sure my Alpina watch and gold ring had been lost forever." She could have added herself to that list. The world of the Nazis was truly insane.

Outside once again, she watched the massive gates swing open. She and others marched numbly back up the hill toward the railroad tracks where she and Betsie had arrived four months earlier. When she reached the crest she didn't look back. Ravens-brück was a nightmare.

"The nightmare is over," she said hopefully.

The group of inmates followed the tracks into the village of Furstenburg. Every moment seemed like a dream to Corrie. Where were the screaming guards? The agony of leather strops? She waited numbly in the small train station with another Dutch woman, Claire Prins, and other inmates. Corrie was numb all the way on the boxcar into the sprawling trainyards of Berlin. Were they really free? It didn't seem possible. Where were the guards?

> **WERE THEY REALLY FREE? IT DIDN'T SEEM POSSIBLE.**

Corrie and Claire clambered into another boxcar, this one on a freight train bound west toward Holland. They learned northern Holland had been bypassed by the British and Americans. It was still held by Nazis. But how else could Corrie have gotten home? She couldn't have gone through battle lines. What if she had been from southern Holland? Would she have died in Ravensbrück? No "ifs," she reminded herself. The boxcars were icy cold. And the two Dutch women had to beg food at train stations. They had no food coupons. Nazis weren't going to waste food on foreigners.

She was getting weak again. She did not indulge in self-pity; she was long past that anyway. She saw now how the German people were suffering under the Nazis. Berlin was near the eastern boundary of Germany, and Corrie traveled across what was once the industrial might of Germany. Her boxcar passed one bombed city after another. As the train passed through the broken, black shell of Bremen, Corrie couldn't help praying for Lieutenant Rahm's family. Some day she must find out if they survived the bombing. Bremen was the closest target in Germany for the British and American bombers.

Magically, one night a man spoke to them in Dutch! She and Claire discovered they were in Nieuweschans in Holland. Not long after that they were rolling into Groningen, where they had to leave the train. The rest of Holland's rail system was destroyed.

Corrie and Claire had become experts at picking the cleanest, most air-tight boxcars. "Oh please, Jesus, don't make Claire and me ever again need that skill," she prayed aloud.

She limped with Claire to a Christian hospital called the Deaconess Home. There Corrie received a strong dose of reality. The young nurse helping her asked, "Where are you from?"

"Haarlem."

"Oh, do you know Corrie ten Boom?"

Corrie blinked. "Are you one of my girls?"

"One of *your* girls? I'm Truus Benes."

"Truus! I'm Corrie."

Truus stared hard. Her face paled. "Of course it's you. I can see that now." She tried to hide her shock. Tears welled in her eyes.

Corrie knew now she was just a shadow of her former self. "Jesus will restore me," she assured Truus.

The Dutch in those dark days considered themselves deprived, but Corrie thought she had found paradise. Her starved senses were glutted. Corrie lingered in a bath, the first warm water on her crusted, flea-bitten skin in a year. The nurses dressed her in different clothes. She was glad to be rid of Nazi clothes she was sure had been confiscated from some poor, confused victim. Her first meal seemed a banquet for Queen Wilhemina: brussels sprouts, potatoes, gravy, even traces of meat. And dessert was pudding with currant juice and an apple. After supper her head sank into a real pillow on a real mattress in a real bedroom. A nurse even propped her swollen feet up on another pillow. The bedroom was a rainbow of colors. And the air smelled so clean.

When she woke up the next morning in her cradle of bliss she saw a bookcase. "Books! Look at the colorful bindings. What luxury."

She heard children playing on their way to school. She heard the merry bells of a carillon and a choir. As she shuffled past a nurse's room on her swollen feet, she heard an organist playing Bach! The nurse was listening to her radio. What a feast life was now! Did it take prison to sharpen these wonderful gifts from God?

Ten days later Corrie got a midnight ride on a food truck. Farmers were trucking their produce illegally all over Holland in darkness. Many Dutch in the cities were starving. Once again the farmers were doing their duty. Finally she arrived at Hilversum. How good it was to see Willem again. Even he, who considered death a mere step into glory, slumped when he heard Betsie was gone. Betsie made everything around her better. Corrie soon learned how much Willem's own family had suffered. Kik had been caught and hauled away by the Nazis. Willem was yellow-skinned. He had contracted some kind of crippling disease of the spine in the prison at Scheveningen. But he was just like Betsie. He acted as if he were going to live another thirty years.

One February day, almost one year since the Gestapo hauled her away from the Beje, she was back in Haarlem. Even though the Nazis still occupied Haarlem, Pickwick delivered her to the Beje

ALMOST ONE YEAR SINCE THE GESTAPO HAULED HER AWAY FROM THE BEJE, SHE WAS BACK IN HAARLEM.

in his limousine. Was this part of the Nazi plan, too? Were they giving privileges back to the movers and shakers like Pickwick so he would not be so vindictive when the war ended?

Pickwick knew far more about the war than Willem. Sitting in the back seat, Pickwick patted her hand. "The armies of Britain, France, and America are poised all along the border of Germany, from southern Holland through Belgium and Luxembourg and France. But they've decided to let the Russians take Berlin."

"Are the Russians in Berlin?" She couldn't believe it.

"Almost." Pickwick smiled. "Yesterday they crossed the Oder River at Furstenburg."

"Furstenburg! That's right outside the camp at Ravensbrück."

"I know."

"Oh, how I wish I could be there to help those poor women when they are liberated." Corrie leaned forward. Soon she would see the Bride of Haarlem, the great cherry tree. But where was it? Had she missed it?

In a sad voice, Pickwick said, "Our great tree is gone. It was a cold winter. Wood was very scarce. You can't go back to Germany, Corrie. There will be plenty for you to do here in Holland."

Suddenly the limousine stopped at the alley door of the Beje. A woman stepped out the door.

"Nollie!" screamed Corrie.

"Corrie!"

Through a flood of tears the sisters hugged each other, while Nollie's daughters gathered around, chattering like happy larks. Cocky, Aty, and Elske hugged Corrie next. Corrie stumbled inside. Yes, the Beje was fine. And it was fine as long as Nollie and her happy girls were there with her. But after they left that afternoon, it was so lonely. The stolen typewriter, rugs, watches, and clocks nagged at her. But what were they compared to poor Betsie? And poor Papa? Grief overwhelmed her. She had to get busy again.

Only days later, a man came to her to ask for help. Corrie had quite a reputation in Haarlem. Could she intervene on behalf of one of his relatives who was in trouble with the Nazis? This man heard there was an official who was sympathetic if approached by someone he knew was in the underground.

"Yes," answered Corrie. "I do know him."

So Corrie trudged to the official's office and asked him clumsily. The official leaped up and shut his door. He was very angry. But his anger faded as he studied her. "Miss ten Boom, you must have gone through hell. You need rest." He smiled. "To put it bluntly, you're not up to this kind of work just yet. You wouldn't want to endanger all the good people in the underground, would you? You know the Gestapo would be delighted to shoot a lot of Dutch people just before they flee. So stay home for a while, Miss ten Boom, and recover your health."

Corrie was ashamed. It was her pride that made her do it. She had gone into the official's office that might have been crawling with Nazis and endangered the very people who were helping the Dutch survive these last days.

"Have I slipped so much in one year?" she asked herself in the mirror. The haggard woman in the mirror confirmed it a hundred times over. The woman had been to hell and back.

She tried to occupy herself with the watch shop. And no ten Boom could tolerate a house with empty beds. She took in a disabled child. But Betsie's vision swelled up inside her. Now was the time. Corrie was back in Haarlem. What was her excuse? Betsie's vision could not be neglected. But where would Corrie find the mansion of Betsie's vision? Even Pickwick did not have a house that grand. And who would she talk to? And who would want to listen? The Nazis were still here.

She began speaking anyway—to clubs, to people in their homes, to anyone who would listen anywhere at any time. Often her contact at a garden club or Bible class would be reluctant, even frightened. But Corrie had to get her message out. It took only a few talks, and she felt God had told her exactly what to say. She had to point out no pit was too deep for someone who was safe in Jesus. She described every degrading detail of imprisonment, so people would know how deep the pit was. She described Betsie's vision. The Dutch must care for these poor people who were scarred by prisons and camps. The Dutch must give them a chance to find Jesus. The Lord would take care of their recovery.

Often a woman would approach her after her talk and whisper, "Can't you wait? There are still Nazis here."

So when a woman, dressed in such finery that she appeared untouched by the war, approached her after a talk, Corrie expected the usual warning. But the woman said, "I'm Mrs. Bierens de Haan. I live in a very large house in Bloemendaal. But now I am a widow. All my sons are grown. My son Jan was taken to Germany. A lightning bolt suddenly struck me that if God would return Jan to me I would have to give up my house for your sister's vision."

Corrie was leery. One does not bargain with God. "Are you sure?"

"It was a revelation, right out of the blue."

Corrie sighed. She didn't want to spurn an offer but what this woman was doing seemed wrong. Corrie said, "My sister had a very specific place in mind." Corrie hoped she didn't sound like a snob. But she wasn't lying about what Betsie said. "This house of Betsie's has a golden floor of inlaid wood. Beautiful manicured gardens surround it. There must be a gallery around a central hall. The walls must be adorned by bas-relief statues. There is a wonderful gabled roof with tall leaded windows—" She stopped. The woman's mouth was gaping. Corrie hoped the woman didn't say too many bad things about her high and mighty demands, her rude ingratitude.

The woman said, "That's my house!"

It was mystical. Corrie was sure now. The woman certainly had not bargained with God. God was using the woman in His plan, just as He used Betsie in His plan, just as He used Corrie in His plan.

Corrie was not surprised when Mrs. de Haan sent her a note later. "Jan came home!" she had scribbled excitedly.

"The home is ours, Betsie," cried Corrie.

So they opened a home for those poor unfortunate minds mangled by the prisons and concentration camps. Holland's liberation seemed almost anticlimactic. Suddenly Corrie realized the Nazis were gone. The streets were full of soldiers from Canada.

> GOD WAS USING THE WOMAN IN HIS PLAN, JUST AS HE USED BETSIE, JUST AS HE USED CORRIE.

They were the Canadian First Army someone told her, under General Crerar. But Corrie was no more interested in details like that than she had been when the German army had arrived. Oh, she knew in her head it was a great day for Holland. But in her heart she knew really great days were when people found the Light.

Corrie seemed to be operating on a new level. Why would God give Betsie such a startling vision if it were not going to come true? This kind of miraculous thing happened in the Bible of course. But now it had happened to Betsie. Corrie was sure of it. She already believed in angels. Hadn't they protected her at Scheveningen, Vught, and Ravensbrück? Would this miraculous foresight ever come to Corrie herself? And it struck her: If she became part of the vision, surely God would tell her what to do next.

To make sure she was deserving, she studied the Bible as she never had before. She didn't want to make any mistakes. One of the first insights she had was that she had to forgive. Everyone. Even the dreadful Nazis. And there were people in Holland whom the Dutch hated even more than the Nazis. Those were the traitors, the Dutch who helped the Nazis. And it was this step in Corrie's burning desire to do God's will that hurt her the most.

In June of 1945, she wrote a painful letter to a Dutchman from Ermelo:

> *I heard that most probably you are the one who betrayed me. I went through ten months of concentration camp. My father died after nine days of imprisonment. My sister died in prison, too.*
>
> *The harm you planned was turned into good for me by God. I came nearer to Him. A severe punishment is waiting for you. I have prayed for you, that the Lord may accept you if you will repent. Think about the fact that the Lord Jesus on the cross also took your sins upon Himself. If you accept this and want to be His child, you are saved for eternity.*
>
> *I have forgiven you everything. God will also forgive you everything, if you ask Him. He loves you and He Himself sent His Son to earth to reconcile your sins. . . to suffer the punishment for you and me. You, on your part, have to give an answer to this. If He says: "Come to*

I HAVE FORGIVEN YOU EVERYTHING. GOD WILL ALSO FORGIVE YOU EVERYTHING, IF YOU ASK HIM.

*Me, give Me your heart," then your answer must
be: "Yes, Lord, I come. Make me Your child." If it is
difficult for you to pray, then ask if God will give you
His Holy Spirit, who works the faith in your heart.*

*Never doubt the Lord Jesus' love. He is standing
with His arms spread out to receive you.*

*I hope that the path which you will now take
may work for your eternal salvation.*

That letter was so painful she was nauseated. Would she meet others who turned her stomach? What if she met a guard who had beaten her? How could she ever forgive a guard for beating sweet Betsie when she was so weak? What if she met a guard she saw beat some inmate to death? What would she do? Could she still forgive? God said, "Yes. You must. Or I will not forgive you." It was right there bright as day in the Lord's Prayer. No one could claim ignorance of that.

She soon discovered that her mind was free of the man who betrayed her family. The hatred, the urge to kill was gone. Once again, God was right. He was always right. Why did people resist Him so? Even Corrie herself resisted Him. She thought long and hard how she must determine God's will for herself. God did not speak to her directly. She was no saint. He did not make it easy for her. Life is not a cartoon. Doors opened and doors closed, and those who had eyes must look hard, those who have ears must listen hard.

One of the first arrivals at the fifty-six-room mansion in Bloemendaal was Mrs. Kan, the wife of the watchmaker in Barteljorisstraat. Mr. Kan had died while in hiding, and Mrs. Kan was very old and infirm. Soon the great mansion was full of patients and volunteers. Corrie still went out speaking her message, once again the organizer finding volunteers and raising money, this time for the rehabilitation center. She made mistakes, like trying too soon to rehabilitate traitors, but she moved ahead. But even Nollie was not prepared for Corrie's next move.

"You're going where?" Nollie asked Corrie in disbelief. "They say it's impossible."

17.
GOING TO AMERICA

I'm going to America," said Corrie.

"But what about the watch shop?" asked Nollie.

"I'm giving the business to my helpers. I tried to get back into the business. I really did. I even traveled to Switzerland for watches, which are very hard to get right now. But I know Betsie would be sad if she knew I was using up my precious time for such things when I could be delivering her message about the victory of Jesus in the concentration camps."

"And the Beje?" asked Nollie.

"I'm turning it into a home for victims of the war. The rehabilitation center in Bloemendaal is overflowing."

"But they say it is impossible to get to America. Everyone wants to go. The waiting list for a passenger ship is a year at least. And you need a lot of money to go to America, Corrie."

"I have fifty dollars."

Nollie, always as blunt as the sunrise, laughed. "Oh, Corrie, dear. What will a pitiful fifty dollars do?"

"If God does not want me to go, the gate will be closed for me. But if He does want me to go, the gate will open."

Nollie laughed again. "Few people pound harder on the gate or more persistently than you do, Corrie. Be sure to write me from America."

And in a time when it was possible only for people with money and influence to find passage to America, Corrie found herself on a freighter just a few days later steaming for America! She didn't worry about her lack of money. She trusted God completely. In New York City she got a room at the YWCA, and every morning she went out, bought her one meal of the day: coffee, orange juice, and a donut, then trudged all day long through the long canyons of Manhattan knocking on every church door. She had to move out of the YWCA and drift from room to room. But a woman who had survived the Nazi concentration camps didn't quit but prayed harder. God would provide for her somehow. But she might have to suffer first.

CORRIE FOUND HERSELF ON A FREIGHTER STEAMING FOR AMERICA!

She struggled. She was operating on nickels and dimes. Some Americans treated her like a beggar. Some told her no one wanted to talk about the war any more. But what were those obstacles to a survivor of the Nazi concentration camps? Corrie began to get a few invitations to speak. Her audiences seemed riveted, especially the Americans who remained at home as civilians. They envisioned the war as battling soldiers not fifty-year-old ladies. How would they have survived an occupation? Corrie prayed her listeners appreciated that she survived on spiritual power.

"But my survival is not my personal miracle at all," she insisted, "but the reality of Jesus!"

She began to meet a few movers and shakers in the American churches. She met a few publishers of Christian books and magazines. She told them she had hundreds of stories to tell. She prayed she radiated the love of Jesus. She got a wrenching letter from Nollie. Willem had died. He had tuberculosis of the spine.

And Tine learned Kik had died in a work camp in Germany. So more of Corrie's beautiful family had succumbed to the Nazis!

By the year's end her first foray into America was complete. She had made some friends she felt she could always rely on, because she intended to came back again. Now it was time to move on. She knew her next move would confound Nollie again. Corrie was going to go to Germany. She and Betsie had talked about it, huddled together in the deadening cold of the barracks. Betsie said they had to go back to Germany and paint the prison barracks bright colors and plant flowers. But that was only the beginning. They had to help the poor, sick guards, the tiny, nasty cogs in the insane Nazi machine, to find new lives through Jesus. Their rehabilitation was important. Any dream of Betsie's was reality to Corrie.

Corrie went to Darmstadt, southeast of Frankfurt, to help a church organization renovate a concentration camp. It was a small but vibrant start. The brightly painted barracks held 160 Germans. Many were women with children. Germany had lost almost four million soldiers in the war. The facts of Hitler's insanity were seeping out, like blood under a closet door, too horrible for the human mind to comprehend. Twenty million Russians and seven million Germans had died. The dead on all sides of the insane war totaled fifty-five million!

The truth about the concentration camps was horrifying, too. In the six years before the war, the Nazis operated camps at Buchenwald, Dachau, Flossenbürg, Mauthausen, Sachsenhausen, and, of course, Ravensbrück. As the war began, these camps held twenty-five thousand political enemies and those Germans the Nazis regarded religious misfits like Jews and Jehovah's Witnesses. But during the war the power-crazed Nazis added camps at Auschwitz-Birkenau, Natzweiler, Neuengamme, Gross Rosen,

Stutthof, Lublin-Maidanek, Hinzert, Vught, Dora, and Bergen-Belsen. Nazis then arrested Gypsies, homosexuals, and prostitutes, too. Millions, mostly Jews, entered these camps from every occupied country of Europe. The Nazis worked them to death and executed them by gassing or shooting. The final toll was over six million!

What many suspected was no longer a secret. "The Nazi devils planned to exterminate every Jew in the world," lamented Corrie. "And everyone else who didn't fit the Nazi mold."

Corrie found out Lieutenant Rahm and his family were still alive. Rahm admitted he still suffered enormous guilt. And Corrie knew millions of surviving Germans carried that guilt. No one needed Jesus more. Once after Corrie talked in a church, the people got up silently, as they always did in Germany, and filed out. But working against the flow was a man coming toward Corrie. He looked familiar.

No! she wanted to scream.

> "I WAS A GUARD AT RAVENSBRÜCK. AFTER THE WAR I BECAME A CHRISTIAN. WILL YOU FORGIVE ME?"

The man stopped in front of her, smiling. "What a fine message, Frau ten Boom. I'm so glad to hear our sins are forgiven." This very man was at Ravensbrück! He was one of the guards who watched coldly as Corrie and Betsie filed past, naked and degraded. She remembered him distinctly. Corrie could not speak. She pretended to be preoccupied. Would he never go away? The man went on confidently, "You mentioned you were at Ravensbrück. You won't believe this, but I was a guard at Ravensbrück. However, after the war I became a Christian. God forgave me. Will you forgive me?" He extended his weathered, hairy hand. It was as repulsive as a snake.

Oh, how hard it is to be in Christ at times like this, thought Corrie. She had a thousand reasons to hate this evil man. Poor, sweet Betsie. But Betsie would have been first to forgive him. Corrie had to forgive him, or God would not forgive her. It was perfectly clear in the Bible. She looked at the man's repulsive hand. Forgiveness was not an emotion one indulged. It was the will of God.

She extended her hand. "I forgive you."

Warmth flooded over her. It was intense. She felt herself glow with love. But it was not her love. She was powerless. It was God's love just as Paul wrote in the fifth chapter of Romans: "And hope maketh not ashamed; because the love of God is shed abroad in our hearts by the Holy Ghost which is given unto us."

Corrie prayed the world would forgive the Germans, too. She bought a German camera and began snapping slides of everything she saw that interested her. As if she didn't have enough to do, she now carefully inked notes on the paper portion of each slide after it was developed. But she remained much more than a tourist.

Theologians who sat around critiquing the Bible but doing nothing to mend broken spirits of their flocks angered her. Once in Germany she said to such a group, "If I speak about the Lord's return, as I probably shall, will you label me a sectarian? If I speak about the fullness of the Holy Spirit does that make me a Pentecostal? Get your labels ready. If I speak about conversion will you label me a pietist? If my message piques your consciences too much, you can label me and set me aside in a dusty pigeonhole."

That was the spitfire Corrie ten Boom. Sometimes her approach was softer. To other theologians she passed out Dutch chocolate before a meeting. Chocolate was very rare after the war. They took it eagerly and ate it. When she finally spoke, she said in mock anger, "No one said anything about the chocolate."

"But that's not true," protested one theologian. "We thanked you for it. I know I did."

Corrie answered, "I meant that none of you asked me how much sugar was in it. Or what kind of chocolate it was. Or the order in which the ingredients were added together. Or the temperature of the mix. Or where it was made." She smiled as her trap was sprung. "You just took it and ate it."

"And it was excellent," joked one unsuspecting theologian.

"And in the same way you should read this!" She brandished her Bible. "Stop analyzing it or you will never be nourished. Pick it up and read the word of God!"

The world did forgive the Germans, as Corrie had. Help poured in to rehabilitate them. After awhile, Corrie saw her own mission in Germany not complete but well underway. There were other places to go to deliver her message about Jesus. She left Germany to continue her odyssey. She knew she seemed wildly impulsive to Nollie, establishing herself and her message in one country and abruptly leaving to go somewhere else. But she was guided by God. Mention of another country would sometimes strike her as divine guidance. It was absolutely compelling. Or a country on a map might seem to jump out at her. And she would have to go there. In weak moments she wondered if her imprisonment didn't make her want her to flee, flee, flee. She no longer took money. Money was not always offered for the right reasons. Nollie didn't want her to take money either. So Corrie became like Paul. She arrived, she worked, she preached the gospel, and she accepted whatever anyone wanted to give her. A bed. A meal. But not money. She proudly called herself a "tramp for the Lord."

For years she traveled alone, brazenly intruding on lives, preaching the gospel: in Cuba, South Africa, Japan, Bermuda, New Zealand, Australia, Spain, England, Denmark, Taiwan, Israel. She returned to America and Germany, too. In America one astonished woman in Hollywood noted Corrie owned only two dresses. But Corrie had Jesus with her. He was more than enough armor.

She wrote books, too. Her anecdotes were becoming very popular. The royalties from the books were pumped into her work. She bought another house in the Bloemendaal district of Haarlem. Of course the house became a center for rehabilitation. She went there only to rest

FOR YEARS SHE TRAVELED ALONE: CUBA, SOUTH AFRICA, JAPAN, BERMUDA, NEW ZEALAND, AUSTRALIA, SPAIN, ENGLAND, DENMARK, TAIWAN, ISRAEL.

occasionally. She was no celebrity anywhere, especially in Holland. Too many others had endured the same experience to be awed by her courage.

Nollie's death in 1953 stunned her. Nollie was only sixty-three. Now Corrie's generation of the family was dead except for herself. She had two episodes in her life when family members died one after another. The first time was connected in her mind to the first world war: Aunt Bep, Aunt Jans, Mama, and Aunt Anna. The second episode seemed connected to the second world war: Papa, Betsie, Willem, and now Nollie. Corrie grieved a long time. In her own way, Nollie was as saintly as Betsie. Six children were Nollie's life's work. Corrie idolized both her sisters.

"Why do I remain?" she asked God.

By 1957, after twelve years of unrelenting activity, Corrie was being crushed under her own popularity. She was in demand. Her books were known far and wide. She had even stayed as Queen Wilhemina's guest at the palace in Holland. Corrie needed help, and she found a perfect companion: Conny van Hoogstraten, a tall attractive Dutch woman. Conny became Corrie's buffer, making traveling arrangements, filtering invitations for speaking engagements, making guests welcome, but protecting Corrie.

Corrie traveled with Conny now: Cuba, Africa, India, Argentina, Korea, eastern Europe, Russia, and countries in every continent. How Corrie loved India. The Indians gathered in the open countryside by the thousands to listen to her. Most of them walked there from afar, and they expected a long speech from the covered platform. Corrie was delighted to oblige. What a change from twelve years earlier in America, when Corrie was taken to a toastmaster's meeting where she was begrudgingly allowed to speak for three minutes!

In 1964 Corrie was brought down by hepatitis. She was seventy, almost the exact age Papa was when he fell prey to hepatitis. Doctors ordered her to rest one year, so she rested at Lweza, a missionary home in Uganda. Located on the shore of Lake Victoria, it was very peaceful. Corrie slept in the same bed every night. Her clothes hung in a closet. She strolled into nearby Kumpala two or three times a week to show people the way to Jesus. Rest was paradise. At the end of the year she did not want to leave. Why should she? She was still leading people to Jesus. This must be God's plan for her.

"Dear Jesus, haven't I earned the right to relax a little?" she asked.

Then she had a visitor.

18.
NO PIT TOO DEEP

Her visitor was a minister from Ruanda, a tiny country also on the shore of Lake Victoria. He said, "Five years ago when you visited us and thrilled us with your prison stories, we could not appreciate the hell you went through."

"Yes?" said Corrie suspiciously.

"We have had a terrible civil war in Ruanda. I myself have been in prison two years. Your message about Jesus sustained me."

"Yes?"

"We would be so happy if you came to minister to our poor people when they get out of prison. Who can do it better than you?"

Once again Corrie packed her bags. God surely did not intend for her to slow down yet. After Conny left her in 1967 to get married, Corrie traveled alone again. She was still going strong, even though she was seventy-five years old. She did buy an apartment in Baarn, Holland, where she was supposed to go periodically to rest and write books. But she did far more writing and receiving friends there than resting. Her personal friends seemed to number in the thousands.

When she was not in Holland, her travels took her places too dangerous for anyone to believe. Who could believe this old lady was in the midst of civil wars in Africa? Who could believe

THERE SHE WAS IN VIETNAM, CRAWLING CREAKILY OUT OF A JEEP TO DELIVER THE GOSPEL TO STARTLED SOLDIERS.

she was so close to the fighting in Vietnam she heard bullets snicking and whizzing through the foliage? But there she was in Vietnam, crawling creakily out of a jeep to deliver the gospel to startled soldiers. She worked with a Dutch missionary named Andrew van der Byl. "Brother Andrew," known widely for smuggling Bibles into Communist countries, was teaching the gospel and ransoming Vietnamese children who had been sold into slavery.

Traveling was harder for Corrie. More and more often she was tempted to quit. Didn't she deserve to rest at her age? And how would she ever replace Conny? Then one day Ellen de Kroon, a tall, blond Dutch woman in her late twenties, visited. Although Ellen seemed so much younger than Corrie, she, too, had scars from World War II.

"We were starving in Rotterdam," she told Corrie. "My father was forced to go to a work camp in Germany. So mother took us to a farm."

"God bless those wonderful Dutch farmers," interrupted Corrie. "What would we have done without them?"

"We five children would have starved. Every time the Nazis came to the farm we all rushed into the woods to hide."

"I must know something, Ellen. Did your father come back after the war ended?"

"Why, yes."

"Praise the Lord. I'm looking for a companion, Ellen. And you seem just perfect," enthused Corrie.

"Me! But you don't know me well enough. I can't type. I can't drive a car. I don't speak German or English."

Corrie was beaming. "You cannot do it yourself anyway, Ellen. But God can do it *through* you."

Ellen agreed to try it. She made some changes in Corrie's life, too. Corrie talked a lot, but she did listen to what other people said. Some were too intimidated by her forcefulness to offer suggestions. But Ellen bluntly said Corrie's wardrobe was outdated. So Corrie meekly let Ellen replace her gloomy wardrobe of long, dark dresses and heavy black shoes. From now on Corrie would wear beige or brown shoes with colorful print dresses.

Corrie was blunt, too. Once after she gave a talk, Ellen criticized something she had said. Corrie suggested Ellen save all negative criticism until the next day when they both could be more objective about it. Another time, when Ellen was whistling as they listened to classical music, Corrie bluntly told her that whistling ruined the pleasure of the music for her.

But Corrie was blunt, not puffed up with pride. Once, after opening mail, she showed Ellen a picture of the very homely mug of a bulldog. "A nice woman named this dog after me, Ellen. What do you think of the resemblance?" Corrie barked to emphasize the resemblance between herself and the bulldog Corrie. After that, she carried the picture in her purse to show everyone her namesake.

"It's a good thing you are a nurse," Corrie told Ellen not long after they teamed up. Corrie had just been in a car accident. She broke not only her shoulder but her right arm in five places.

Ellen helped her rehabilitation. Corrie could not write with her shattered arm, so she practiced until she could write with her left hand! Later she worked with sand bags to build the strength back in her right arm.

"Not bad for an old lady of seventy-five," bragged Corrie.

But to Corrie the temptation to quit was still strong. Traveling tired her. Speech after speech tired her. And after every speech, she and Ellen sat at a table selling her books and tapes. She still would not ask for money but earned her way just as Paul had earned his way making tents while he evangelized. Corrie noticed her tired mind drifted into self-pity more and more often. But then she got terrible news that Conny had died of cancer. How could Corrie quit when vivacious Conny had spent so much of her youth to help her spread the gospel?

And Corrie would meet people who seemed true saints, like a Lithuanian woman and her husband in the Soviet Union, where religion was strictly forbidden. The woman was twisted grotesquely by multiple sclerosis. Each morning her husband would feed her breakfast, prop her in front of an old typewriter, and buffer her on all sides with pillows so she wouldn't fall over. Then the woman would wind paper after paper into the typewriter and peck out translations of the Bible into Lithuanian, Latvian, and Russian. The woman translated Bibles right under the noses of the Communists. Who could ever suspect such a hopeless cripple?

After seeing saints like that woman and her husband, Corrie would say, "I'm going to die in the harness for Jesus."

> ### "I'M GOING TO DIE IN THE HARNESS FOR JESUS."

Years of speaking in public taught Corrie how to assemble a talk in seconds. All she needed to know was how much time her hosts were going to allow her. She had two favorite props for her shorter talks. One was a piece of material she called the "crown." She would begin by holding up what appeared to her audience to be nothing more than rough blue cloth with tangled knots of golden thread hanging from it. She would recite a poem:

My life is like a weaving
between my God and me.
I do not choose the colors
He works steadily.
Sometimes He weaves sorrow
and I in foolish pride
forget He sees the upper,
and I the underside.
Not till the loom is silent
and the shuttles cease to fly
will God unroll the canvas
and explain the reason why
the dark threads are as needful
in the skillful weaver's hand
as the threads of gold and silver
in the pattern He has planned.

Corrie would triumphantly flip the cloth over to show her audience what God sees: a golden crown on a field of blue! That is what the believer will eventually see of God's plan in heaven. Even the most sophisticated listeners seemed stunned by the metaphor.

Then she would unashamedly launch her appeal, "Do you know Jesus? I don't mean do you know *about* Him—but do you *know* Him? I asked the Lord Jesus to come into my heart when I was five years old. He came into my heart and He has never let me down. . . ."

Another favorite prop of Corrie's was a flashlight. She would throw the switch, and when the light failed to shine, she exclaimed, "Is there no light in your life?" She unscrewed the end of the flashlight. "Invite Jesus into your life!" She pushed a battery into the flashlight. The light still failed to shine. Her audience was startled.

"What's wrong?" She unscrewed the end again. "What is this?" She pulled out a rag. "Pride!" She pulled out another rag. "Envy!" She pulled out another. "Love of money!" Finally she would slide in the battery again. The flashlight beamed brilliant light!

She had hundreds of stories she had polished over many years. Sweet Betsie taught her how to enchant listeners in the beginning. But now Corrie had the powerful story of the concentration camps, too. "No pit is too deep when Jesus is in your heart," she said. And she knew that when she told this story she became more than a peppery old lady telling charming stories. The world now knew the Nazis were devils. How many in her audience could have survived the Nazi camps? How many of them could have shed the bitterness like she did? Surely they knew she got her courage from Jesus just as she said.

> "NO PIT IS TOO DEEP WHEN JESUS IS IN YOUR HEART," SHE SAID.

One day Corrie asked faithful Ellen, "Do you remember this passage from chapter fifteen of 1 Corinthians: 'Be ye stedfast, unmoveable, always abounding in the work of the Lord'?"

"I remember it well," said Ellen agreeably.

"And do you also remember chapter one of 2 Timothy: 'For God hath not given us the spirit of fear; but of power, and of love, and of a sound mind. Be not thou therefore ashamed of the testimony of our Lord'?"

"I remember it as well," answered Ellen suspiciously.

"Good, because you are going to have to start speaking to the public."

"What!" Ellen was terrified. What was Corrie doing to her? She had learned to type. She had learned to drive a car. She had picked up a smattering of English and German. How much could one person do?

But soon Ellen was giving speeches. Sometimes Corrie was simply too exhausted to give another speech. And the speech was already scheduled. They couldn't let an audience down. The message was too important. When Ellen overcame her fear it was not so difficult. Corrie insisted Ellen need not feel like a fraud. Ellen had truly suffered under the Nazis, too.

Through her grinding travels Corrie was well known but not a celebrity by any measure. But all that would change.

19.
TRAMP FOR THE LORD

A writing team told Corrie how excited they were by her book about Ravensbrück called *A Prisoner and Yet*. But they were sure there was a bigger story to be told. Soon Corrie was collaborating on a book with them emphasizing her war experiences from 1939 to 1944. The book was to be called *The Hiding Place*. The title referred to two hiding places: the secret room where the ten Boom family hid refugees from the Nazis, and Jesus, in whom Corrie hid when events were crushing her. Published in 1971, the book was no narration of dry facts, but a first-person cliffhanger.

Corrie, still globe-trotting with Ellen, now lugged along dozens of copies of that book on her trips. Any moment was a perfect occasion for Corrie to unashamedly spring her book on any candidate for salvation. That included everyone.

To a skycap taking her bags through an airport Corrie would say brightly, "You really know your way through this airport, don't you?"

The skycap would humor her, "I sure do, ma'am."

Corrie would ask bluntly, "Do you know your way to heaven?" And no response brought her next move. She would pull out a copy of *The Hiding Place*, sign it, and present it to the stunned skycap.

Laughing about it later, she would say to Ellen, "If only I could be there after he reads it to hear him say, 'That old lady went through all that?' But best of all, now he may find the way to Jesus and heaven."

Corrie was relentless with her book. She passed out thousands of copies—free. What were books for? And so what if she paid for the copies herself?

The evangelist Billy Graham told Corrie he was interested in making *The Hiding Place* into a movie. He had a motion picture company called World Wide Pictures to make movies with Christian themes. Corrie prayed that it would come true eventually. But she had too many other activities to think about it much.

> BILLY GRAHAM TOLD CORRIE HE WAS INTERESTED IN MAKING *THE HIDING PLACE* INTO A MOVIE.

Also as a result of the book she was invited to appear on Robert Schuller's *Hour of Power* television show. She was told she was the best example he could find of a person who had suffered persecution for the Lord. After that first appearance on nationwide television, her invitations to speak increased more and more.

By 1974 Corrie had collaborated with another writer on a sequel to *The Hiding Place* called *Tramp for the Lord*. American friends had to incorporate her as "Christians, Inc." to free her of red tape and the necessity to manage her money. Corrie still traveled the globe. Money meant little more to Corrie than buying airfare for Ellen and herself to their next destination. After all these years, she perfectly understood her papa's total disregard for money.

By 1975 Billy Graham's World Wide Pictures started filming

The Hiding Place. Locations were in England and Holland. Veteran actors assured a professional effort. Arthur O'Connell, nominated for two Oscars in a long Hollywood career, was to play Papa. Julie Harris, a veteran of Hollywood and Broadway, had the role of sweet Betsie. Eileen Heckart, winner of both an Emmy and an Oscar, would play an older version of the scrounger Mien. Broadway actress Jeannette Clift had the part of Corrie.

Corrie shrugged off any credit for the film. "It's another way to let the world know Betsie's vision."

That same year, she finished collaborating on a third major book, *In My Father's House,* covering her early years. Billy Graham invited her to speak on his televised Crusades. She suspected he thought she needed to be reined in at eighty-two, but he did convince her that personal appearances were no longer the most effective way for her to spread the gospel. They were necessary at the beginning of her calling, but now they actually limited her impact. Her impact would be greater through his televised Crusades.

But she still wanted to travel the globe and talk to groups, too. Spreading the message "Jesus is Victor" was so personal that way. And in Tel Aviv, she presented the two millionth copy of *The Hiding Place* to another brave woman, Golda Meir, the prime minister of Israel. How excited Papa would have been to see such a meeting.

Early in 1976, Ellen left Corrie to be married. This time Corrie's companion was an English woman, Pam Rosewell. She joined Corrie resting at her new house in a suburb of Haarlem. Shortly after Pam arrived, Corrie had a nostalgic golden reunion with her club girls. Corrie was amused. Pam would soon discover that the work never ended, and just when Pam thought she had everything under control, Corrie would take on something else. Imagine Pam's surprise to learn eighty-four-year-old Corrie had planned an eighteen-city tour in America, lasting seven months!

But things had really changed for Corrie, too. Now she had fans. Fans were celebrity worshippers. They would rush up and explode a flash bulb right in her face. Or a flash would blind her right in the middle of her presentation. "Please don't do that," she would protest. "This is about Jesus. Not me." Even those rude symptoms

EIGHTY-FOUR-YEAR-OLD CORRIE HAD PLANNED AN EIGHTEEN-CITY TOUR IN AMERICA, LASTING SEVEN MONTHS!

of her growing popularity with fans were not the worst. "Watch out for the neck-huggers," grumbled Corrie after awhile to Pam. And Pam would try to fend off fans who would try to grab the eighty-four-year-old around the neck to hug her.

As much as she enjoyed the warmth of personal appearances, she finally admitted to herself this new kind of exuberant fan was dangerous to her at her age. She had a troubling dream now, too. She was locked in a room with no way out. Were her prison miseries haunting her? Corrie brushed off the disturbing dream and made her plans. She was convinced now she must channel her flagging energies into short films and writing books. Personal appearances were too dangerous, and she was not reaching enough people that way.

She told Pam she wanted to move to the Los Angeles area in California, close to the headquarters of Christians, Inc. in Orange and close to Billy Graham's movie studio. Thirty-three years to the day since she was arrested by the Gestapo in 1944 she moved into a ranch style home in Placentia. She dubbed it "Shalom House," for her desire for peace and quiet, and soon celebrated her eighty-fifth birthday there.

After talking to both World Wide Pictures and Bill Barbour

from her publisher, Corrie announced her plans to Pam: five books and five movie shorts. Pam protested. How could Corrie do so much? Was this peace and quiet? Corrie told her again the story about the girl in her childhood who scoffed at her sixteen plans and winked. But Corrie really did intend to write five books and make five movie shorts. If only Pam could keep her from taking too many other commitments.

But of course Corrie did make other commitments. It was only natural after she finished her short prison film, *One-Way Door*, that she start a neighborhood group praying weekly for prisoners. Naturally she had to be at the prayer meeting herself. And when she got an invitation to the prison at San Quentin, how could she refuse to go? And when people showed up at Shalom House saying God sent them there, how could Corrie refuse to see them? Pam watched helplessly.

By December Corrie had finished the first of her five books, *Each New Day*, and stopped long enough to get a pacemaker. She was proud of her new constant pulse of seventy-two. She was sure the pacemaker would serve the Lord well. One night, before bed and after reading about people who claimed to have seen the glory of God, she said to Pam, "Tonight I'm going to ask the Lord if I can see His glory." About midnight she had a vision of Jesus. She asked Him if she could see His glory and He answered "Not yet." After she asked "Are you coming soon?" He answered "Yes, but not before you come to heaven."

After that revelation, Corrie, who prayed every day, "Father, let that great day soon come when Your Son comes on the clouds of heaven," just like her Papa ten Boom had prayed, never expected to be alive when the great day came.

She celebrated her eighty-sixth birthday while making a film with Christian Indians in Arizona. In the summer of 1978, she made a third film, *Jesus is Victor*, and was honored in Denver on an episode of "This is Your Life" for television. Each venture now required more recuperation. And recovery was difficult at Shalom House, where Corrie couldn't refuse to see anyone.

Often Corrie saw fatigue or botched plans as an attack by the devil. "Let us pray," she cried to Pam. "The devil knows that his time is short. We are not fighting against flesh and blood but against principalities and powers. There is a devil, much stronger than I, but there is Jesus, much stronger than the devil, and with the help of Jesus I will win!"

Following an unrelenting schedule, Corrie reached her goal of five books and five movie shorts in less than two years. But one morning in August, when she woke up she couldn't move. Was she only dreaming she woke up? In her heart she knew she was awake. All her memories of Mama's paralysis flooded back. Now here was Corrie sixty years later. Her troubling dream of being locked in a room had come true.

> **CORRIE REACHED HER GOAL OF FIVE BOOKS AND FIVE MOVIE SHORTS IN LESS THAN TWO YEARS.**

20.
NINETY-FIRST BIRTHDAY

Soon after she was rushed to the hospital she lost consciousness. How long she drifted in the void she couldn't tell. Gradually she realized she was awake again. When she tried to speak she must have been speaking gibberish, because Pam just looked at her blankly. Soon she realized she was saying a few words like "yes" and "Conny." She remembered how she dismissed the importance of her own name sixty years ago when Mama said it after her stroke. Had she been Mama's favorite like Conny was her favorite? She never knew that until now.

Weeks later, back at the Shalom House, Corrie now played the guessing game with Pam, just as Mama had played it with her. Corrie would gesture yes or no to question after question until the answer she sought finally came.

Occasionally she recovered full speech.

One day Pam said to her, "I'm sorry, Corrie; I know how much you dislike ladies wearing pants, but I must wear slacks today."

Corrie could see Pam expected indifference or a polite nod from the wheelchair. Somehow she found it in herself to snap, "Why would you want to do that?"

Startled, Pam explained, "I can't seem to find a dress or skirt that's clean."

"Rubbish!"

But Corrie's life now was mostly a pleasant indulgence. An old friend of Corrie's, Lotte Reimeringer, came to help Pam. The two helpers walked Corrie in the garden behind the house. She watched birds at the bird feeder. She did needlework. She listened to Bach. Her favorite Bible, the English translation by J. B. Phillips, was read to her several times a day. She prayed with Pam and Lotte. She received only a few visitors. She went on drives in a car. She was able to put together another devotional book with Lotte by indicating her choices of many clippings she had saved over the years. But the old peppery evangelizing days were over.

And sometimes she wept in frustration. *Why keep me here so long, God? Why?*

But she would remember Mama's paralysis and her unbound love. Love triumphs over all afflictions. And our earthly sufferings only serve to make that which awaits us an even greater glory. And so she poured out her love to Pam and Lotte and everyone around her.

WHY KEEP ME HERE SO LONG, GOD? WHY?

Then she was struck down again. It was May 1979. And yet, again she lived, more helpless than before. Her hearing was still very sharp. Well-meaning friends discussed her funeral and burial. Pam already knew what Corrie thought of burial. "Oh, just bury me in the back yard," she had said with a wave of the hand. As the inevitable neared, her attitude had not changed. Her body was no more than a worn-out, cast-off shell. The real world was the spiritual world that awaited, just like Jesus said.

She heard hospital staff say she weighed no more than eighty pounds. She heard it said she showed the first symptoms of kidney failure, a certain precursor of death. That angered Corrie. God would decide when she had to leave her body. She started getting better.

"What a marvel!" exclaimed Pam.

The doctors no longer liked to make predictions about eighty-eight-year-old Corrie ten Boom. She seemed to be getting higher medical help. She returned home again. She was completely bed-ridden now, her speech almost nonexistent, her arms and hands rags. During a Bible reading she might raise her arms to heaven if a truth struck her forcefully. She astonished Pam one day when she adjusted a pendulum clock with one quaking finger.

But mostly she lay immobile as Lotte and Pam entertained her. They played Bach for her. They read the Bible. They prayed with her. They read her own books to her. They even let a few visitors see her. In the evenings, they gave her slide shows of the sixty-six countries and hundreds of dear friends she had visited. She had seven thousand slides! How fortunate she had been. She seemed to have lived a dozen lives. But occasionally the futility of her existence overwhelmed her and she wept. *Why keep me here so long, God? Why?* And then she would remember Mama and her suffering and the indescribable glory that awaited the faithful. The next moment she was radiating love again to Pam and the others.

In the fall of 1980, she suffered a third stroke. She became even less responsive. Why was God doing this to her? What was the point? Yet Corrie had dealt with such troubling questions before. Hadn't she taught disabled children? Corrie felt shame. How could she question God's plan? This had happened to Mama. She must not forget the glory that awaited. But still, why did she linger so long?

One day she had a marvelous vision of the Lord. It seemed as rich as Revelation. It had to be the third paradise Paul could not write about. How she wanted to at least tell Pam and Lotte that she glimpsed glory. But could she? She couldn't depend on even one or two words these days. Corrie pointed toward the wall.

"Do you want to hang some more pictures?" asked Lotte.

Corrie shook her head.

"Is something wrong with the wall?" asked Pam.

Corrie closed her eyes in exasperation. She prayed for Pam and Lotte.

Pam laughed. "The old spitfire is still there," she said to Lotte. "I saw Corrie work with people in the old days. Sometimes if they didn't understand her she would just stop and bluntly pray out loud, 'Oh please, God, give this person the wisdom to understand what I mean.' That's what she is doing to us right now."

Corrie opened her eyes. She managed to say, "Amen."

Lotte pointed to a picture of Jesus. "Are you telling us something about the Lord?"

"Yes!"

"Is He showing you His glory?"

"Yes! Yes!"

Corrie lived on and on. She experienced visions. She experienced despair. Eventu-

"IS HE SHOWING YOU HIS GLORY?"

ally, Corrie could not open her eyes. She had nothing left but her hearing. She heard Pam reading Psalm 103, a Dutch tradition for birthdays: ". . . who redeemeth thy life from destruction; who crowneth thee with lovingkindness and tender mercies." That verse seemed written for Corrie. And it was as if Betsie was reading it to her.

Later in the Psalm, she heard more words that seemed especially for her:

> *Like as a father pitieth his children, so the LORD*
> *pitieth them that fear him.*
> *For he knoweth our frame; he remembereth that we*
> *are dust.*

> *As for man, his days are as grass: as a flower of the*
>   *field, so he flourisheth.*
> *For the wind passeth over it, and it is gone; and the*
>   *place thereof shall know it no more.*
> *But the mercy of the LORD is from everlasting to*
>   *everlasting upon them that fear him, and his*
>   *righteousness unto children's children;*
> *To such as keep his covenant, and to those that*
>   *remember his commandments to do them.*

Never were these words more poignant for Corrie. Surely it was time at last for the Haarlem flower to turn to dust. But the Lord's love was everlasting to everlasting. And, as if God offered her passing as one more proof of His will, Corrie passed away on April 15, 1983—her ninety-first birthday.

FOR FURTHER READING

I. Five books in particular cover Corrie ten Boom's life from childhood to her "silent years" (roughly in the following order):

Ten Boom, Corrie with Carole C. Carlson, *In My Father's House.* Old Tappan, New Jersey: Fleming H. Revell Company, 1976.

Ten Boom, Corrie, *Prison Letters.* Old Tappan, New Jersey: Fleming H. Revell Company, 1978.

Ten Boom, Corrie, with John and Elizabeth Sherill, *The Hiding Place.* Old Tappan, New Jersey: Fleming H. Revell Company, 1971.

Ten Boom, Corrie, with Jamie Buckingham, *Tramp for the Lord.* Old Tappan, New Jersey: Fleming H. Revell Company, 1974.

Moore, Pamela, *Five Silent Years.* Grand Rapids: Zondervan Publishing House, 1986.

II. Other books of significant interest are:

Carlson, Carole C., *Corrie ten Boom: Her Life, Her Faith.* Old Tappan, New Jersey: Fleming H. Revell Company, 1983.

Stamps, Ellen de Kroon, *My Years with Corrie.* Old Tappan, New Jersey: Fleming H. Revell Company, 1978.

Ten Boom, Corrie, *Father ten Boom.* Old Tappan, New Jersey:
Fleming H. Revell Company, 1978.

III. Other books by Corrie ten Boom, mostly devotional:

*Amazing Love, Each New Day, Clippings, Defeated Enemies, Not
Good If Detached, Marching Orders for the End Battle, Plenty for
Everyone, A Prisoner and Yet. . .*